HOW TO WRITE FAT POSITIVITY

AN INCOMPLETE GUIDE

Salt & Sage Books

SALT & SAGE BOOKS

Cover designed by Blue Water Books

eBook ISBN 978-1-7349234-8-3

Paperback ISBN 978-1-7349234-9-0

To authors who fiercely write real people as real people.

STATISTICS

Statistics provided reflect available information in the United States of America. We recognize that these statistics are exclusionary by nature, and encourage you to take a look at worldwide statistics to get a broader picture, particularly if your story is not set in the United States.

LETTERS FROM THE AUTHORS

Dear Reader,

I'm glad you're here and ready to learn more about how to write fat characters in a positive way.

Stories tell us how to feel about each other and ourselves. Here's how stories about fat people have affected my story:

When I was little, I went to the theater with my family to see *The Goonies*. The character Chunk is an example of what has been normal for our culture: a negative portrayal of fat children, fat families, relationships with food, and what the normal social response to those three things ought to be.

I remember my trimmer older brother pointing to the screen as the movie once again bullied Chunk for our amusement, and as other people in the theater laughed at Chunk, that older brother elbowed my other brother in his soft middle, and said, "Look, it's you."

Suddenly my middle brother wasn't someone who loved math, who was great at building sand castles, who loved reading *Encyclopedia Brown*— he was fat. He was just fat. He wasn't just a person anymore, he was a fat person. And fat, the movie further explained via Chunk's on-screen antics, also was synonymous with clumsy, odious, and not too bright.

I remembered that moment a few years later when my body prepared for puberty by gaining some weight, and we watched *The Goonies* again. *That's me*, my brain said with shock. *We are also an unlovable, unsightly butt of a joke. That's us.* The horror bloomed within me as I realized that I no longer had the same place in the world I'd had before. I wasn't like the other kids anymore. I was different because I was fat.

It wasn't just me getting this message, either— the bullies at my school and in my family also understood the approval these stories gave to others to bully me into making my body more acceptable. The fatphobia was so universal, even family who meant well saw the pain society had in store for me, and warned me against making myself so unlovable. The cumulative lesson was clear: I owed it to everyone and to myself to look different.

Like so many of us voracious readers, it was during painful times in childhood that I turned to books for respite. For years the shelves of the school library had been my refuge, and once people weren't safe, I turned to books to find friends. Unfortunately, they weren't much better. I tried to find a representation of me, an example of how someone like me could still live life and be acceptable, but I didn't find that representation that I ached for.

Whether it was Judy Blume's *Blubber*, Roald Dahl's *Charlie and the Chocolate Factory*, or even my still-beloved *Baby-Sitter's Club* series by Ann M. Martin—these books all repeated what I heard on TV, at school, from family and friends: My body was wrong. My body was unacceptable. I wouldn't be considered worthy, or powerful, or disciplined, or beautiful, or strong, unless my body looked like the thinner bodies that were universally preferred.

I felt imprisoned, not by my own body (which actually was just a normal amount of prepubescent pudgy) but by the persistence of this painful, dehumanizing story about what fat bodies mean about who fat people are.

Nobody wants to be without story, me especially! I knew I wanted to be a writer by the time I was seven, years before my body became unacceptable, and my life was books. So, like any other human whose basic belonging is on the line, I launched into decades of struggle for my own story, for the right to be represented even just in my own head.

I spent years dwindling in anorexia, for which I received glowing praise and support. I compulsively exercised and missed out on opportunities to just be a happy child with a normal social life because I couldn't afford to risk gaining weight and losing people.

Bodies hate starvation, though, and after years of restrictive eating, my metabolism rebounded with relentless weight gain, my body telling the true story that I'd subjected myself to famine for over twenty years. I became exactly the fat adult that I'd spent years terrified of becoming, and I've journeyed through life in a body of fluctuating weight since, noting with care the huge differences in how others treat me and tell my story based solely on how much I weigh.

I wish I'd had good stories, loving stories, with respectful and positive representation. What I read made it clear that I could not be even a side character, let alone a protagonist, unless I had a different body. I was too fat for my story to be allowed to start, or for it to be about anything other than my journey towards reaching the minimum level of acceptable to the people around me.

Stories are teachers—whether they teach torment or refuge is up to the teller.

You, dear writer, have the opportunity to help create stories for real people to inhabit. You have an opportunity to make sure your story grants kindness and tells the truth, and the truth is that all bodies have worth, and all people deserve to live their own stories.

Thank you for taking your storytelling power seriously.

Sachiko Burton

Dear Reader,

Thank you so much for taking the time to purchase and read this guide. Fat positivity is a difficult but crucial topic to explore. We are taught through mainstream media that to be fat is to be unhealthy, weak, ridiculous, and more. If there's a negative human quality to be included in a story, odds are multiple writers have used a fat character to represent it. Too often we see ourselves portrayed as greedy villains, slapstick sidekicks, mindless eating machines, or desperate souls hungry for love (and cake).

Unpacking the many ways in which our society is constructed to be harmful to fat people is no easy task, but not for lack of material. We have enough experiences and insights to create a multi-volume series on the subject of how to write fat positive characters alone, but this is an "Incomplete Guide" for a reason. We aren't here to teach you everything. We're here to show you just how much there is to learn and provide resources to help you do so.

This is an opening door—an invitation to see things from the point of view of multiple contributors who will share their hurts, their insights, and their requests that writers be more mindful, more intentional, and more committed to representing fat people authentically and respectfully.

I hope you listen. I hope you come away from this experience with the tools and resources you need to build stories that make room for more than just our bodies. I hope you see us as the gloriously unique and worthy individuals we are.

Kimberly Vanderhorst

Dear Reader,

I never thought of my weight, or fat in general, until one moment I can remember as a preteen, when I was ten or eleven years old. I had just gotten out of the van and stood there, looking down at my round stomach, realizing how much it bothered me that it stuck out and touched my shirt. I couldn't wait until I grew breasts so my shirt would hang straight down from them.

That's where my fatphobia and the road to eating disorders started. And my mom, bless her, unknowingly reiterated my feelings about my body by, among other things, always saying that she would wait to buy clothes until she lost weight. She unknowingly taught me that a fat person wasn't worthy of taking care of. Wasn't worthy of having more than one or two skirts to wear. Was only worthy of existing to serve everyone else.

Don't get me wrong—I love my mother dearly. She is a hero to me in so many ways. I only wish she'd learned much younger how valuable she was and how much she deserved to take up space regardless of her body size.

I now have a daughter and three sons. I know the messages I've sent them haven't always been the right ones. Even though I've actively tried not to talk about fat negatively in front of them, I know they can see how often I'm uncomfortable in my own body, and it pains me greatly that they may have ever absorbed any of my own self-image. But in working on accepting myself, and helping others see that they are deserving of space and respect, I hope that my children will learn the same. I hope this guide will help you not only create more authentic fat characters, but help you see how similar everyone really is, regardless of what they look like.

Rebecca Blevins

WHY THIS BOOK?

Dear Reader,

Welcome to *How to Write Fat Positivity*, part of Salt & Sage Books' Incomplete Guide series. We're glad to have you here!

Do you remember the first time you read a book and thought, "Ah! That's me!"? That ringing inside of being seen?

I do. As a child, I was obsessed with a Cinderella book my Grandma had given me. Cinderella was white, blond, and female, just like me. I was probably two.

When we started doing interviews for Salt & Sage, we asked, "When have you felt seen?" The answers we've heard from our incredible editors & readers have been inspiring and heartbreaking. Some of them have been avid readers their whole lives, but have yet to read about someone who looks like them, feels like them, talks like them. Some of them shared instances where they hadn't been seen, and even more shared stories of how what they read, watched, or heard was actively harmful to them.

Fast forward to 2019. Salt & Sage Books was born basically overnight. It rapidly grew from there, and one of Salt & Sage's most popular services is a sensitivity read. We are really proud of the sensitivity reading services we provide. We've worked hard to create an inclusive, diverse, and safe place for our readers and editors to thrive. Salt & Sage is all about quality editing with kindness—and kindness isn't just an encouraging edit letter or complimentary in-line notes. Kindness is helping authors like you (like me!) who want to do better and be better, but aren't sure where to start. That meant providing a level of sensitivity reading beyond a basic rubber stamp of yes/no.

As I read through the sensitivity reader letters, I noticed a pattern: the same concerns were appearing again and again in the letters from our Black readers. I saw the same pattern from our trans readers. Once I noticed it, the pattern showed up everywhere: our sensitivity readers were regularly rehashing the same concerns related to their identities.

This got me thinking—if our authors were consistently having the same issues, could we help in a more focused way? And what about the authors for whom a sensitivity read is too expensive?

The more I thought about it, the more I liked the idea. I've talked to lots of people in the writing world about writing diversely, and the same thing stops nearly all of them: fear. They don't know where to start. They aren't sure that their Googled information is accurate. They don't know anyone who they can ask, or they are too nervous to ask.

After lots of brainstorming about the best way to provide this information, the Incomplete Guides were born. You're currently reading our Incomplete Guide about how to write fat positivity. This was written entirely by our editors who are fat. They've addressed the most common areas of concern that pop up in their sensitivity reading. You'll see sections where they write from their own point of view. Multiple authors have contributed to each section. Some of them have included their names; others have chosen to remain anonymous for their own safety. (Doxxing is still a very real concern, and one we actively try to protect our editors against.)

Of course, even though this was written and edited by multiple editors and sensitivity readers who are fat, we called the guide *incomplete* for a reason—it's not a blank check, nor is it a rubber stamp. Even if you address everything in this guide, you should still seek input from at least one fat person. Salt & Sage Books has sensitivity readers on staff, but many creatives also have success posting about their specific needs on Twitter's writing hashtags. Be sure to pay your readers for their labor. Listen carefully to their feedback, and you will most certainly write a better story.

We hope that *How to Write Fat Positivity: An Incomplete Guide* will be a helpful resource as you write fat characters. We invite you to step inside the viewpoint of our editors and sensitivity readers experience a deeper, more impactful form of researching. We hope that will help you confront your own biases when writing fat characters.

Mostly, we hope that you will continue to create thoughtful, nuanced characters, and worlds that reflect the reality of living as a fat person. We hope that you will be part of the movement to create more diverse books and other creative content. It's critical work. It's occasionally difficult. It's deeply worth the effort.

May you write books that help people feel seen.

Yours,

Erin Olds

she/her

CEO, Salt & Sage Books

FATPHOBIA AND FAT SHAMING

F atphobia, put bluntly, is the fear of fat people, which includes a person's own fear of "getting fat." Fat shaming is when people shame others—or themselves—for being fat.

When did fatphobia and fat shaming come into play? Sadly, much of it began with racism in the early 1800s. Let's take a quick look at some of the history behind fatphobia to help us understand where it comes from.

FATPHOBIA'S HISTORY

You may be surprised to learn that back in the early 19th century, about a hundred years before the medical establishment began being concerned about what they view as excess weight, slimness wasn't historically about health. Fatphobia began because of biased, wrong, and hurtful assumptions about people of color. "In the West, it's actually rooted in the trans-Atlantic slave trade and Protestantism. In the trans-Atlantic slave trade, colonists and race scientists suggested that Black people were sensuous and thus prone to sexual and oral excesses. Protestantism encouraged temperance in all pleasures, including those of the palate. By the early 19th century, particularly in the U.S., fatness was deemed evidence of immorality and racial inferiority."[1]

Even though fatphobia in the Western world began with racism, it has grown to include people of all races and genders. We use the term *fat* to mean slovenly, lazy, disgusting, evil, bad, smelly, and as an insult. (More on this in other sections.) When people go to a high school reunion, they might present weight loss as evidence they're no longer the "fat kid." Or conversely, they'll see a former bully who used to have what they would describe as the "perfect body" and think, "Good—they got fat" as if it's some sort of comeuppance.

As a society, we think that getting fat is horrifying and/or embarrassing, and that fat existing on our bodies needs to be hidden, removed surgically, or dieted away. Our society's fatphobia is so extreme that the weight-loss industry in the U.S. alone is worth about $71 billion dollars.[2]

One of the most commonly cited reasons for losing weight is improving health. While it's true that carrying extra weight can contribute to certain types of health issues[3] (note I said "contribute," as many people have similar health issues unrelated to weight), an almost 40-year-long study of over 100k people in Denmark shows that a person who is overweight may actually be healthier and have a lower mortality rate than a person of "average" weight.[4]

What's significant about this? People often say that they're concerned about someone's health as an excuse to fat shame them As if that gives a person license to harass and make judgment calls under the guise of false concern.

Is it okay to treat a fat person poorly because we believe they "brought it on themselves by being fat"?

No. No, no, no, *no*. A person is a person is a person, regardless of their size, and should be treated with respect—not because of what they look like, but because they *exist*. A person's risk of health issues or lack of risk thereof is irrelevant—no one's value should be determined by their body's propensity for storing calories or the effect that propensity has on them. *Fat shaming is never justifiable, even out of concern—false or real—about a person's health.*

The Problem with BMI

Fat people are judged incredibly harshly not only by the world in general, but also by medical professionals, who are overwhelmingly fatphobic. Having a high Body Mass Index, or BMI, is a red flag in the medical world. Even the U.S. Centers for Disease Control and Prevention utilizes the BMI tool to screen for obesity, or levels of fatness.[5]

So let's talk BMI for a minute, and how that factors into fatphobia.

Did you know that the concept of BMI was based on the Quetelet Index, invented by Adolphe Quetelet, a mathematician who lived in the early 1800s? It was a way to measure the mass of a person since Quetelet wanted to figure out exactly what the average man's size was.

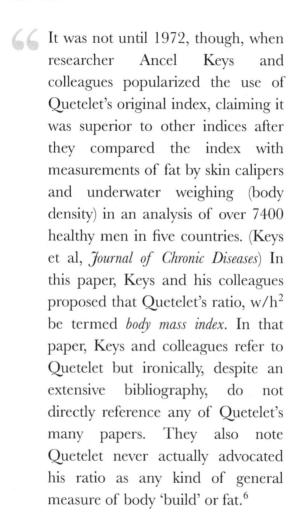

> It was not until 1972, though, when researcher Ancel Keys and colleagues popularized the use of Quetelet's original index, claiming it was superior to other indices after they compared the index with measurements of fat by skin calipers and underwater weighing (body density) in an analysis of over 7400 healthy men in five countries. (Keys et al, *Journal of Chronic Diseases*) In this paper, Keys and his colleagues proposed that Quetelet's ratio, w/h^2 be termed *body mass index*. In that paper, Keys and colleagues refer to Quetelet but ironically, despite an extensive bibliography, do not directly reference any of Quetelet's many papers. They also note Quetelet never actually advocated his ratio as any kind of general measure of body 'build' or fat.[6]

This means BMI was based on an index that analyzed a man's body composition—which we know is different than a woman's. "For its inventor, the BMI was a way of measuring populations, not individuals—and it was designed for the purposes of statistics, not individual health."[7] Yet the medical profession holds nearly everyone to the BMI standard.

Now, recording accurate levels of body composition can be important—but the value judgments that come along with a high BMI are not okay. If doctors are going to record body composition, they should use tools that actually work! And they shouldn't assume a high BMI automatically means someone is unhealthy. We must look at blood tests, blood pressure, and other tests that are better indicators of health. Athletes have had doctors tell them to lose weight for having a "high BMI" when their numbers are inflated because of the levels of muscle they carry. Many people, including doctors, use weight = health to justify fatphobia.

But what if someone *does* have an illness that is directly related to how much fat is in their body? Doctors should record the data and help the patient without judgment.

Being. Fat. Is. Not. A. Moral. Failure.

Period.

Fat People Can Be Fatphobic

I personally have experienced my own internalized fatphobia combined with someone else's. I had an eating disorder as a teen and was both gratified and disheartened when an older guy I had a huge crush on told me my body was "almost there." Genetically I always had a little belly, so my abdomen wasn't perfectly flat, even at the low end of my "acceptable weight range." He was nearly approving of my size only because I had an illness I wasn't being treated for. I looked healthy and fit when I had an eating disorder because I was scared to death of being fat. I got kudos for my body size when what I needed was a mental health professional to help me overcome my extreme internalized fatphobia. Even as I got older and gained the equivalent of another one of myself, then eventually lost much of that weight, I still had so much internalized fatphobia. Even when I was fine with other fat people, I hated myself for being fat.

Living in your own fat body when you battle fatphobia isn't any fun. Having moments of hating your body because it's fat does absolutely nothing except help you hate yourself. That's the exact opposite of what anyone with those feelings should be doing. Fat people deserve love just as much as thin people do. *People deserve love.* That's it. No other qualifiers.

I deserve clothes that fit my body. I deserve to love myself even if I'm still battling my own internalized fatphobia. My body is worthy even though I gained back all the weight I lost. I'm worthy of love, I'm intelligent, I have much to offer. I'm not lazy or a slob because of the way my body looks and behaves. I don't deserve to die because I "let myself get fat," as is so often the message the world gives me.

Please, *please*, check yourself when it comes to fatphobia. Writers, please stop assuming that because someone is fat that they have a low IQ, don't know how to eat (I know more about nutrition than most people I know), are lazy, have health issues because they're fat, or are a drain on society. It can be hard to love yourself when society tells you that you're too disgusting to exist, when doctors overlook serious health concerns because you're fat, when *fat* is used as an insult.

Stop attaching judgment to the word *fat*. Like *skinny* or *thin*, *short* or *tall*, saying "they're fat" should be a description, not an insult.

It's time to end fatphobia.

Story Implications

Check every character for fatphobia, and yourself as the writer. Often, fatphobia creeps in very subtly. For example, I often see fat people as the villains, or dumb, or the IT guy slouching in his chair with grease stains on his belly, cheese puff crumbs all over his shirt, and candy wrappers on the floor. I see fat people who are arrogant, smelly, gross, and are usually either single or the cuddly mother/grandmother type. We'll talk more about these stereotypes in Chapter 9 and Chapter 10.

Remember that fat people can be beautiful, fall in love, have great sex, don't need thin friends to give them makeovers (they *can* be fashion mavens!), can run marathons, run up a flight of stairs without getting breathless, and don't always need to be the funny fat friend. Give your stories fat characters without making them caricatures, and I highly recommend hiring sensitivity readers and finding beta readers specifically for fatphobia. Be part of the solution when it comes to treating fat people as valued members of society.

1. https://www.universityofcalifornia.edu/news/fat-phobia
2. https://reportedtimes.com/status-report-of-the-u-s-weight-loss-market-in-2020-effects-of-the-pandemic/
3. https://www.health.harvard.edu/staying-healthy/can-you-be-overweight-and-still-be-fit
4. https://www.sciencealert.com/the-healthiest-weight-might-actually-be-overweight-massive-study-finds
5. https://www.cdc.gov/obesity/adult/defining.html
6. https://www.psychologytoday.com/us/blog/the-gravity-weight/201603/adolphe-quetelet-and-the-evolution-body-mass-index-bmi
7. https://elemental.medium.com/the-bizarre-and-racist-history-of-the-bmi-7d8dc2aa33bb

2

FALSE EQUIVALENCIES

In this Guide, we've chosen to divide false equivalencies from stereotypes. Stereotypes, which most creatives are familiar with, are oversimplified ideas of people and their behaviors. False equivalencies are along those same lines, but instead they are a logical fallacy, where when someone sees "fat person," they also assume something else. For example:

Stereotype: fat people eat all the time.

Many of the false equivalencies relating to fat people are ones that can be so subtle we hardly notice they're used—unless we've had fat equivalencies pointed out to us. Along with this, fat people often feel a great deal of shame for being fat (not always, but often enough to be an issue), so may feel that false equivalencies are "normal" or "just the way the world works." Many fat people may feel an undercurrent of rightness when reading thinly veiled insults in a book or seeing those insults played for a laugh in the media because they may say a lot of those things to themselves, even if they don't realize it.

Case in point: I recently read *Dumplin'* by Julie Murphy. During the book I kept feeling a little off and unsettled. Like something was wrong with the main character, Willowdean, because while she did feel self-conscious about her body when kissing a boy she liked (a boy who was considered so hot he basically looked like a movie star), she didn't really seem to care about her body shape otherwise. The book also sent the message (spoiler alert) that it was tragic that her aunt died because she was "deathfat" (so morbidly obese she couldn't do anything but watch TV all day) and also portrayed another fat girl as whiny and stereotypical, which sadly, felt like a normal portrayal to me, since I'm used to fat people shown as irritating.

It really got under my skin that Willowdean's lack of being self-critical bothered me so much, and that the guy she liked didn't care that she was fat. There was *finally* a character modeling the very behavior I was trying to cultivate in myself and teach my children, so why was I experiencing such cognitive dissonance about it?

I finally realized why—because while I've been actively challenging myself and trying to change my thoughts, the false equivalencies of *fat = undesirable, fat = unacceptable,* and *fat = failure* have been branded into my brain for so long that it's going to take a lot more exposure to media with body-positive characters to weed them out.

An additional contributing factor to these and other false equivalencies is that fatphobia and fat judgment are still largely an acceptable form of stigma and discrimination in our society. Not only are fat people viewed as subpar, we are encouraged to hate ourselves unless we shrink our bodies to a size that makes others feel comfortable when they look at us.

Let's discuss a few false equivalencies.

FAT EQUALS STUPID

How often do we see the trope of the stupid fat kid? Or the stupid, mean, fat bully? How about the fat girl/woman who is stupid enough to sit in a wobbly chair that then breaks? Or the fat dad on sitcoms who is so stupid no one knows how he manages to keep himself alive?

This false equivalency also translates to the myth of "Weight loss is simple. Calories in, calories out." This myth implies that fat people are too stupid to know how to lose weight. Weight-loss reality shows have unhealthily demonstrated the wrongness of that myth. People have different genetic makeups, frames, hormones, many things that affect how their bodies process and store fuel. In spite of this, many people believe that fat people are too stupid to know what causes weight gain, and that stupidity must filter into all areas of our lives, so we become caricatures to laugh at.

Here's the truth:

Most fat people know more about nutrition than the average person.

Not all fat people can lose weight.

Not all fat people *want* to lose weight.

Fat people can be smart, stupid, and everything in between. But we have far too many characters in media who are written as the "stupid fat person."

Fat Equals Lazy/Sedentary

How often do people comment on a picture of a fat person, assuming that person sits around on their "fat ass" every day? One of the most common myths about fat people is that we're lazy. That we never exercise and just sit around all the time.

The truth is that most fat people have full and active lives.

It's not fair to assume fat people don't exercise. And if they don't exercise, it's not right to assume it's because they're lazy. If a fat person has a disabled-parking sticker on their car, some people assume it's because they're too lazy to walk—when in reality, they have a medical condition or injury that makes it difficult for them to park farther away. Doctors and DMVs don't hand out those parking stickers like Halloween treats.

You can't tell someone's physical fitness level just by looking at them. Many fat people exercise a lot. They may walk for exercise or run marathons. Plenty of thin people have chronic illnesses or are unable to exercise, but most people won't sit on a bus and make a judgment about how they should ride a bike instead of riding the bus.

When I was in my mid-30s, I started trying to get "back in shape." It wasn't long before I realized that something was really wrong with me. So I went to the doctor, and he put me on medication and told me to walk for a mile a day.

I started walking again and began needing multiple rest days between. I went back to him and told him that something still wasn't right, and he told me to increase my walking. I found another doctor.

A few years later, after some serious health challenges, I discovered I have an incurable genetic condition that—you guessed it—has severe fatigue and body pain as part of the routine symptom list.

Unfortunately, fat-shaming in the medical establishment is an epidemic. Psychology professor Dr. Joan Chrissler said, "Research has shown that doctors repeatedly advise weight loss for fat patients while recommending CAT scans, blood work or physical therapy for other, average-weight patients."[1]

Don't assume a fat person can't exercise. If they don't exercise, don't assume it's because they're lazy or enjoy sitting on their behinds all day. And if you see a fat person exercising, don't automatically assume they're doing so because they're trying to lose weight. They may be doing it for their cardiovascular system or to build bone or muscle or endurance, or to help strengthen their immune system, or because they enjoy moving their body. Their being fat isn't an invitation for others to speculate or comment on their reasons for exercising.

Fat Equals Hungry/Greedy

Probably the first character that comes to mind when I think of fat = hungry/greedy is in Roald Dahl's *Matilda*. Bruce Bogtrotter is an 11-year-old overweight boy who steals a slice of Miss Trunchbull's cake and as punishment, is made to eat a huge chocolate cake—which he does, to her surprise—because *of course* a fat boy could eat a giant chocolate cake in one sitting. (If I sound a bit cynical, forgive me; it's because I am.) This theme is repeated often in media: Dudley Dursley in *Harry Potter and the Sorcerer's Stone*, Augustus Gloop in *Charlie and the Chocolate Factory*, Monica Geller as "Fat Monica" in the TV show *Friends*, etc.

In reality, when it comes to food, not every fat person eats a large amount. Some have metabolic issues and don't eat as much as their "thin" counterparts. Still others are fat solely because of medical conditions that make them gain weight and have zero to do with food or willpower.

If a fat person does overeat, it is more likely to be in private. They generally won't be the ones scooping the last slice of pie from the table or eating noisily or sloppily. Many fat people are uncomfortable eating in public because of that misconception, as they know people tend not only to watch them eat—but how much and how often. I'll be straightforward with you—I'm one of those fat people who are often uncomfortable eating in public because someone might be judging how much I'm eating or what I'm eating (A burger and fries? She should know better. A salad? Oh, at least the poor thing's trying). *Ugh.* On the other hand, there are fat people who don't care what anyone else thinks about their eating habits. My goal is to someday be like them!

Fat people are often accused of not having any willpower when it comes to food. Interestingly, scientists have found a gene that, when switched off, doesn't send people the signal that they've eaten enough food. For those people, the hunger signal stays on and so they eat more than those in whom the gene is working normally. For people who have the opposite problem, the gene stays switched on, which means they're not hungry when they should be.[2]

Both extremes can wreak havoc on a person's metabolism, promoting weight gain. If a person doesn't eat enough, their metabolism slows, and then when they eat "normally" they're more prone to weight gain.[3] And what about the person who keeps losing weight and regaining it, and their friends judge them for their "poor willpower"? A fat person's body chemistry changes, so even when they lose weight, their bodies fight to get back to the size they used to be.[4] Judgment is unhelpful and in fact, is downright harmful to your fat friends and family.

Fat Equals Smelly/Poor Hygiene

I know someone who had the stereotypical fat, smelly, male roommate who never showered. I also know a man who is fit and attractive by most standards, but he rarely showers and therefore smells awful much of the time. But which man is going to have his hygiene blamed on his physical attributes rather than his lack of hygiene? The fat guy.

Yes, fat people do tend to have extra creases that can develop a smell, just like any place on the body that can be subject to dampness and therefore, bacteria. We fat people do things to help reduce the chance of that happening: we shower regularly, dry off well, wear clean clothing, use deodorants/baby powder in various places. Yet even when we do these things, people will still assume we smell.

A few years ago, psychology professors at UCLA did a study that proved people in general had fatphobia because they associated bad smells with fat people. How did they do this? People were told to expect a scent along with a picture, but the *smells were not actually there.* And sadly, some of the very harshest judges were themselves obese, which is interesting to me for one reason—I'm always worried about whether or not I smell, even if I've recently showered and there's no way enough time has passed to build up any unpleasant scent.

A. Janet Tomiyama, an assistant professor of psychology at UCLA and coauthor of the paper said, "There are no checks and balances on weight stigma in the way you would see with racism, sexism or homophobia."[5] Since racism, sexism, and homophobia are still epidemic in our society, you can imagine how rough the world can be on a person who is fat and falls into one or more of those marginalized categories. For example, fat Black women are overwhelmingly subjected to substandard and negligent medical care.[6]

STORY IMPLICATIONS

These are only a few of the false equivalencies that fat people encounter. I encourage you to do more research and to not only avoid false equivalencies in your own writing, but to actively counter those false equivalencies. Have a fat romantic lead? Make them smell good to the romantic interest. Let your fat characters eat normally, like most people do, without calling attention to their chewing patterns or having them drop food all over themselves. Show your fat characters going for a walk to get fresh air or lifting weights to build muscle without making it about losing weight. Make fat characters smart and intelligent without being villains. Give your fat characters fashion sense and style without always making it loud or quirky.

---

1. https://www.apa.org/news/press/releases/2017/ 08/fat-shaming

2. https://people.com/health/scientists-discover-gene-mutation-that-prevents-obesity/
3. https://diabetesstrong.com/why-not-eating-enough-food-can-make-you-gain-weight/
4. https://www.independent.co.uk/life-style/health-and-families/health-news/there-s-no-point-telling-obese-people-exercise-more-doctors-claim-10039641.html
5. https://www.latimes.com/science/sciencenow/la-sci-sn-obesity-smells-foul-20150320-story.html
6. https://rewirenewsgroup.com/article/2018/10/12/fat-black-womens-bodies-are-under-attack-why-did-it-take-a-thin-white-man-to-get-our-cries-heard/

3

PHYSICAL HEALTH AND FATNESS

W e know the scenario well—a character's life is in shambles, hanging by threads of self-neglect at best and self-loathing at worst. The problems at the center of the story range from lack of social acceptance or romantic love to mental/physical health concerns to lack of respect in their professional lives.

Whatever the issue, and whatever the path forward, what we also know is that at least part of the story-presented solution will likely be weight loss. Whether our hero/heroine requires a montage of sweaty jogs in the park or a series of scowls at veggie-filled plates, the primary message is the same: being anything but thin is not only at the root of life's problems, but it's also something that could have been controlled all along. The deduction? Your weight—and, therefore, your problems—are all your own fat fault.

Even if the stories are unrealistic in other ways, this attitude manages to slip easily into individual and societal acceptance. The door is wide open for it to do so as our modern patterns of thinking throw shame at body sizes and shapes labeled as outside the norm, no matter how many times we hear that the average U.S. woman exists in the so-called "plus size" realm.

While this way of thinking is damaging in a multitude of ways, one that is only recently coming under examination is the idea that fatness automatically equals a lack of care about health—the idea that if characters could only want it badly enough, they could achieve a thinner body—and, therefore, better health. It's just one sweaty montage away.

How often have we seen fat characters with an active lack of care for their health? An obsession with unhealthy food and disdain for exercise are the calling cards of many a fat character. This is usually played for laughs and offset by a journey, whether past (*Friends'* Monica or *New Girl's* Schmidt) or yet to be embarked on (*Bridget Jones'*

Diary). It gives the impression that fatness is not only funny but rooted in a disregard for self.

This idea of fatness coming from neglect is perpetuated by programs like *The Biggest Loser* which play off the idea that, if individuals would just care and work hard enough, weight loss is not only inevitable, but the best prize one could seek. This is further enforced by the unhealthy practices utilized to garner the extreme results that are the show's calling card and the shaming thrown at the contestants.

"The show's rationale was the logic of abuse: 'I'm doing this for your own good. I wouldn't have to do this if you didn't make me.' This, after all, was the price of thinness."[1]

Again, the message is that fatness equals a choice.

Let's talk about that choice.

As one who has spent the majority of my life fat, there have been times in which I have tried desperately to choose thinness. There seemed to be a plethora of ways to do so. However, whether through shortcut products or good old diet and exercise, I never could shed that pesky BMI level identifying me as obese. But, regardless of its size, I was fortunate to have a body that allowed me to exercise and general health unrestricted by allergies or nutritional limitations. And as I took advantage of that, I gained a love for caring for my body. I began learning about exercise science, nutrition, and general wellness. What I learned changed my life—but, not my size. And I couldn't help but ask myself, much like Stephen Blair, a professor at the Arnold School of Public Health at the University of South Carolina, "Why is it such a stretch of the imagination," he said, "to consider that someone overweight or obese might actually be healthy and fit?"[2]

Obesity has been my constant companion through the last decade of 5-6 days-a-week workouts that run the full spectrum of strength, cardio, and flexibility. It takes in green smoothies and salads bursting with lean protein and organic veggies. It walks—and runs!—with me on sturdy legs, is held up by the strong, flexible spine that comes from years of yoga, and is framed by squared shoulders usually at least a little sore from my last upper body workout. And if obesity feels at home in the same body that can take in and put out all these amazing things, who am I to make it my life's work to dismiss it like the plague society tells me it is?

I won't pretend it hasn't been difficult to navigate a world stacked against this belief. As established, media—even in its most noble attempts—does a great job at undermining it. But science is a wonderful ally. In her article "Better to Be Fat and Fit Than Skinny And Unfit" Tara Parker-Rope states, "Several studies from researchers at the Cooper Institute in Dallas have shown that fitness...is a far better indicator of health than body mass index. In several studies, the researchers have shown that people who are fat but can still keep up on treadmill tests have much lower heart risk than people who are slim and unfit."[3] Stephen Blair reiterates "instead of focusing only on weight loss, doctors should be talking to all patients about the value of physical activity, regardless of body size."[2] And, returning to the concept of fatness being a choice associated with laziness and lack of drive, obesity researcher Natasha Scvey of the Uniformed Services University of the Health Sciences speaks specifically to this: "We know from a lot of really good research that obesity is not as much in an individual's control as we think it is. People talk about willpower—that's a very small part of the equation."[4]

Physical health experts can also be fantastic allies within this thought process. Rebecca

Simms, certified yoga instructor and owner of Cedar Yoga Space in Cedar City, Utah, United States, shares the following insight in relation to yoga—often represented as an activity for thin people: "Yoga is not one size fits all. You cannot change your body to fit a yoga pose, but you can change a yoga pose to fit your body. My goal as a teacher is to create a specific recipe for each student in their own bodies and their own practice. As soon as we let go of what this should look like and stop comparing ourselves to the person next to us, we can begin moving with joy in our body, begin showing gratitude for the way our skin feels and bones move to create space where we need it."

So, if many experts agree that accepting and moving within the space our body requires is a positive thing without the stipulation that smaller is better, why does this stereotype prevail? Sometimes it is readily believed because "even good people" perpetuate fatness as the ultimate failure. Once I sat in a meeting with other leaders of my church congregation in which it was joked that, "in heaven," food won't have calories, so thinness will be automatic. I was the only fat person in the room and also seemed to be the only one concerned that, without calories, we would also be lacking basic energy to accomplish work, holy or otherwise. But it's only a joke, right? Well, aside from the joke's insensitive nature, that situation was one of many in which I have found myself both the fattest *and* the most health-conscious individual in the room.

We also often believe the stereotype because many who are viewed as experts in their field still default to the idea that thinness equals health. Fat individuals are forced into roles of fierce self advocacy when they're denied thoughtful medical treatment due to faulty assumptions and/or prejudices.

When a lack of weight loss accompanying my long-term healthy lifestyle landed me in a doctor's office seeking reassurance that every-thing in my body was as it should be, I explained my lifestyle in detail to the specialist. I left that office with a recommendation to eat the kinds of foods I had already told him I was eating, take up an exercise regimen much like the already-adopted one I had already described to him, and a prescription for an appetite suppressant I didn't need. Because I pushed, I also got a script for full blood testing.

To my relief, my blood work showed that my health was top notch. To my disappointment, it was clear that, regardless of any discussion, all my doctor saw in my situation was a fat female who hadn't yet found the willpower to fix what he saw as her biggest problem. The worst part? My experience is the rule rather than the exception when it comes to my fat peers.

If the universal keepers of health are perpetuating this message, how can the media really do any different?

But we must.

CHARACTER AND STORY IMPLICATIONS

Because you are reading these words, I know you share in my desire to bring a different face to fat characters across all stories. Let's leave behind the protagonists pursuing weight loss as the gate to happiness, let's move beyond the fat friends used as comic relief. We can hang a lantern on thin main characters' misconception of fatness and allow them to arrive at more truthful conclusions, much like in Gail Honeyman's *Eleanor Oliphant is Completely Fine*. At the beginning of the story, Eleanor—a thin person —is critical of fatness while referencing what she was taught about it during her childhood.

But as the story moves forward, she comes to examine her abusive mother's judgment regarding the health of those who look differently than she does.

We can also go a step further in portraying protagonists whose fatness is not a plot device. In Meredith Tate's *The Last Confession of Autumn Casterly*, teenager Ivy has hobbies and interests, family relationships and struggles, friends and love interests, and while her fatness is referenced (a nonchalant, "Yeah, I'm fat now," in response to a friend's mom who hasn't seen her in a couple years), it is no more important to the story than her eye color. There are no disclaimers regarding her food choices or activity levels. This is the kind of representation we want to see when it comes to fat individuals in a story.

Maybe your fat characters hate working out but do it because there's a history of heart disease in their family. Maybe they love it but can't do it because of an invisible illness. Maybe they love vegetables because they grew up helping their grandpa with his garden. Maybe they hate the taste and texture, so they drink them in green smoothies. Maybe they dislike all traditionally healthy food but function well anyway. The bottom line? Fat people are no different from thin people in that they are all different; that is, like thin people, fat people will have varying activity levels and attitudes towards health. Each of them.

Can weight affect health? Sure. Can health affect weight? Absolutely. But, as evidence supports, laziness regarding health is not something that automatically comes with being fat.

So, let's keep the laziness out of our writing by giving our fat characters rich, complicated, diversely healthy lives!

———————————————

1.
2. https://www.nytimes.com/2008/08/19/ health/19well.html
3. https://www.gadsdentimes.com/lifestyle/20080819/ better-to-be-fat-and-fit-than-skinny-and-unfit
4. https://www.nbcnews.com/health/kids-health/brain- differences-may-be-tied-obesity-kids-study-says- n1098446

LIVING IN A STRAIGHT-SIZED WORLD

You may be scratching your head, asking yourself, "What are the stereotypes surrounding fat characters and fashion?" I'll help you out—there aren't many. Why? Because, when it comes to portraying fat people buying, wearing, and enjoying clothes, storytellers often take the same approach they do with most things in the realm of fatness— make it funny, make it invisible, or make it sad.

In this particular case, that means the options are over-the-top or too-small (funny), frumpy or not mentioned at all (invisible), or beautiful clothing that doesn't come in the right size (sad).

While thin characters' clothes are notable on the screen and described in detail on the page, fat characters' approach to fashion is nearly nonexistent. Beyond the problematic-but-prevalent belief in the fashion industry that fat bodies are just not as fun or interesting to dress lies the consequential truth—shopping as a fat person is, therefore, truly not as fun or interesting either.

Think about it: you can probably list a handful of memorable shopping montages from movies —in preparation for a date, a dance, a new job, or a big life change, an individual shops to poppy tunes, trying and rejecting dozens upon dozens of options thrown at them by sales associates and friends.

Now, think again: how many of those montages feature individuals shopping so-called "plus size" or "big and tall" threads? Why does the number drastically diminish?

The answer is easy: shopping while fat is hard.

I don't think anyone would argue with the fact that the fashion industry is problematic. But for fat people, the retail clothing industry *is difficult to access at best, and downright abusive at worst.*

In an interview with *InStyle* magazine, actress Aidy Bryant discussed attempting to create an interesting yet accessible plus-size wardrobe for her character Annie in her tv show, *Shrill*: "Initially, I felt strongly, like, 'Ok, I want these to all be things that exist and things that she could afford,'" she admits. "Then, pretty quickly, I was like, you know, this is a real opportunity to have a plus-size lead who is dressed equally as cool and with as much style as every lead, on every TV show, on every channel for years. So that, yes, we could have done something where my character only is wearing Forever 21 Plus and all that stuff. Or, we had an opportunity to make an impression and create someone who *could* exist if fashion would meet that [need]."[1]

The article states that Bryant and her team created designs for Annie from scratch with the kind of access to resources and professionals that, of course, the average person of any size does not have. But unlike her thin counterparts, Annie's real-life relatables have no way to recreate the same kind of fit and fun in clothing seen on-screen.

"The fact that Annie's wardrobe isn't replicable in real life is kind of the point." Bryant notes that, even as an individual with privilege, she encounters the same frustration regarding dressing and shopping that many of us do.

With as much progress that has been made in the plus-size market, the breadth of choice is really not there...I could probably name on 10 fingers the big places you can shop, and even then, it's just... it's complicated. You're still having to hunt, in a way, for anything that's different.[2]

Another challenge when it comes to the act of shopping while fat, making it particularly different from how we see retail outings portrayed in the media, is that shops are not set up with us in mind. While, yes, there are a handful of stores among the thousands of retailers that cater to our size, most places banish clothing of larger size—and, therefore, people of the same—to a distant, dark corner. Department stores are split into straight-sized designer-based sections sprinkled with ideal lighting and well-thought-out product placement while the handful of those designers who create plus-sized garments are all grouped together in an afterthought of a corner, usually on a different, less-traveled floor altogether.

Not only that, many store dressing rooms are not designed with fat customers in mind. When you have to press yourself against the far wall and suck in your stomach just to close the dressing room door, you definitely don't feel welcome there.

What does this mean for shopping trips usually portrayed as social, jovial outings with friends? It means your friends better be fat too, or you're going to be leaving them with their lattes and luxurious setup on the first floor while you ride the escalator to rummage through afterthoughts.

Even if you do find something perfect for you, actually wearing the clothes you managed to find is another tough one. Because, just like shopping, wearing clothes while fat is hard.

In an article for *Refinery 29*, Eliza Huber states, "Oftentimes, the integrity of the design of a piece will get distorted as it gets graded to a larger size, either because proportions aren't carefully considered or because extra seams or panels are added to accommodate a larger body. Some of these changes are necessary to maintain proper fit, but it is a shame when the original design of a garment is compromised."[3] It's equally a shame that designers aren't seeking to accommodate fat bodies in their original designs.

This is the experience of larger bodies every-where—even when we manage to find some-thing interesting in our size, it's not likely that our size and shape was actually taken much into account when making the garment. Most likely, the designer simply decided to add more mate-rial instead of actually adjusting for fit.

And this isn't limited to clothing. Accessories are affected by the limited mindset of designers as well. Alyssa Kaplan, the founder of The Scrunchie Club, an accessories brand that caters to womxn and non-binary people of all sizes—conducted a survey last year that showed that 95.3% of women (96% of the 275 respondents identified as plus-size) have experienced trouble shopping for boots that fit their calves. [4]

The founder of popular plus-size lifestyle and fashion blog The 12ish Style Katie Sturino told *The Zoe Report* that "the current state of size inclusivity within the jewelry industry is almost non-existent."[5] She went on to explain that while the industry has "bigger fish to fry," there's still a "clear need for extended sizing in jewelry. Every item that is available in straight sizes should also be made available in extended, and I know there's a market for this just like with clothes." Even handbags, which are often misconstrued as one-size-fits-all, need to up their game when it comes to cross-body styles and shoulder bags. Huber says it well in the opening paragraph of her article: "The fashion industry doesn't much care about dressing plus-size women, and it shows in the options it provides for them."[6]

You might ask why this matters—why put so much stock in one part of life that many people feel is frivolous? (Note: it's only frivolous if you don't have to worry about it.)

First, we all exist as part of society. Whether that society is broken or not, it's where we live. And, as examined by Eliana Dokterman for *TIME 100*, "[Women] are more closely scrutinized for what we wear. When we get married or interview for a job or play professional sports or run for President of the United States, we encounter a whole set of standards and expectations. We can be shamed for an outfit that's too slutty, too dowdy, too pricey—take your pick. That's the burden women carry into the fitting room. And when we can't find clothes that fit, let alone clothes we like, it can be infuriating."[7]

While women are particularly impacted by this, it's important to note that frustrating sizing—and sizeism—affects all genders. Because of the double standard noted by Dokterman, most of the research and thought surrounding this concept does focus on women, so those are the statistics we have to work with. Ideally, in the future, we will see more studies and conversations revolving around how other genders are affected by the sizeism power plays in the fashion industry.

For example, "a women's size 12 in 1958 is now a size 6. Those numbers are even more confusing given that a pair of size-6 jeans can vary in the waistband by as much as 6 in., according to one estimate. They're also discriminatory: 67% of American women wear a size 14 or above, and most stores don't carry those numbers, however arbitrary they may be."[8]

Dokterman's expression of frustration of "as if it's somehow *my* fault that I'm not short or tall or curvy or skinny enough to match an industry standard. I hate that it feels like nothing fits" is mirrored by fat individuals everywhere including actress Melissa McCarthy who states, "It's like we've been taught we all should have third eyes, and if you don't have a third eye, what's wrong with you?"[9]

Why else put stock in the role of fashion in everyday life? Some of us just really, really like it. Just like putting a piece of art on a wall gives an individual the opportunity to both see and be seen on a deeper level, to express their tastes and style, putting on a piece of clothing affords the same exciting opportunity. For some, clothing is merely viewed through the lens of function— and there is absolutely nothing wrong with that. There is also nothing wrong with it being a means of art and expression. And that opportunity should be available to all.

***

CHARACTER AND STORY IMPLICATIONS

So, what does this mean for your fat character?

It means that, no matter how much or little they are interested in fashion as expression, they have been affected by society's prejudice when it comes to the clothes they wear. And since we all have to get dressed every day, whether we're interested in what the mirror shows or not, it's affecting them.

If they go shopping, they will encounter evidence of prejudice in what's available, where and how it's displayed, and the gaze of retailers and other shoppers. When they get dressed, they will encounter some degree of effect of the fashion industry's unrealistic and inappropriate view of the shoulds and should nots of bodies. And, because very few individuals are completely sheltered from the harmful views of those attempting to affect how we feel about our bodies, they will be measuring themselves—or trying very hard not to—against unrealistic standards of beauty.

Shining a light on these challenges is a great step, as is shining a light on fat fashion altogether! Avoid having thin friends give fat characters makeovers, as if fat characters automatically have no fashion sense of their own, and steer clear of using fat fashion as a humor device.

If it feels true to your character to center a laugh or two around something in this area, hang a lantern on it by allowing a side character or the POV character themselves down the line to call for a reexamination. Give your fat characters the same breadth you would thin ones in how they feel about clothing—look at how thin characters are described in regard to this and practice applying it to fat ones. Some love clothes as art, some view them as a neutral necessity, but all are experiencing what we discussed above regarding fashion options and societal views.

One of those views we want to work hard at eliminating, though many who utilize this approach are well-meaning, is characters who are good or acceptable "in spite of being fat." This appears on the page often as characters described as having pretty features disassociated from the bulk of their body (most often their facial features), female characters described as "curvy" (not all fat people are), fat characters whose clothing detracts in some way or "fixes" their bigger body in some way, or anything on the page that implies there are one or more traits or choices making the fatness of the character more acceptable.

Practice writing in a way that paints physical traits of characters and how they're dressed in clothing or accessories as neutral—because, whether society says so or not—that's exactly what they are.

---

1. https://www.instyle.com/fashion/aidy-bryant-fashion-interview-shrill-season-2-outfits
2. https://www.instyle.com/fashion/aidy-bryant-fashion-interview-shrill-season-2-outfits
3. https://www.refinery29.com/en-us/2020/08/9980813/plus-size-fashion-shopping-frustrations
4. https://thescrunchieclub.com/
5. https://www.the12ishstyle.com/
    https://www.thezoereport.com/p/why-plus-size-jewelry-is-still-hard-to-come-by-in-2019-17297230

6. https://www.refinery29.com/en-us/2020/08/
   9960057/coronavirus-plus-size-inclusivity-fashion-
   industry-effect

7. https://time.com/how-to-fix-vanity-sizing/

8. https://www.wsj.com/articles/why-womens-clothing-
   sizes-arent-what-they-used-to-be-11558690200

9. https://time.com/how-to-fix-vanity-sizing/

5

MENTAL HEALTH

Being bombarded, often daily, by fatphobic messages that suggest you are lazy, ugly, unhealthy, and generally of less worth than people whose bodies take up less space than yours can be extremely harmful to your mental health. Hardly a revolutionary statement, is it? And yet, this is a reality far too many fat people are forced to inhabit.

Untangling the many ways in which physical and mental health interact is no small challenge, and isn't the ultimate purpose of this chapter. But hopefully it will provide you with some insights that might be helpful to you in pondering the many ways in which mental health can play a role in your fat character's life.

First and foremost, we want to caution against the false equivalencies that fat = mental health issues, or that mental health issues = fat. The topics discussed in this chapter are relevant to *some* fat people—not all. Be wary of accidentally incorporating overgeneralizations like these into your story. Many fat people have the joy and privilege of experiencing mental wellness, though few are completely unaffected by the pressures of fatphobic culture.

THE BRAIN BODY CONNECTION

In discussing the brain-body connection it's important to establish that the brain is a physical part of the body. While both our society and our medical communities differentiate between "Physical Health" and "Mental Health," the brain has a physical presence just like our heart, lungs, and pancreas do. And just like those other organs, the brain is susceptible to illness and malfunction.

Where things begin to get a bit wobbly is when we try to envision a physical home for our minds —the place where our thoughts, emotions, and sense of self reside. The notion that the entirety of who we are is housed in a physical organ of the body is unsettling to many of us. Separating the physical and the mental aspects of health is one way in which we try to make sense of it all.

Unfortunately, that separation is the source of multiple misconceptions about mental health. If we take the physicality of our brains out of the picture, that leads to people being held responsible for the impact of physical functions completely outside their control. Can you control your serotonin levels with a mere thought? Of course not. And yet, that's basically what people are suggesting when they try to cheer up a clinically depressed person with cheery platitudes.

Yes, the sun will indeed come out tomorrow, but that won't address the physiological needs of a depression patient.

Much like fat people, those with mental health conditions are subjected to countless layers of stigma, the pressure of which can ultimately worsen their mental health. In fact, there's a great deal of overlap with regard to the kinds of questions/suggestions that pour in from well-intentioned (or not so well-intentioned) bystanders:

- "Have you tried X?"
- "My friend/neighbor/coworker tried Y and she's never been happier/healthier!"
- "Just stop doing Z and you'll feel better."

This overlap becomes particularly harmful for fat people with mental health conditions because now there are *two* things for people to blame us for. We often hear one-two gut punch statements like:

- "No wonder you're depressed—you're not taking care of yourself. I wish you would..."
- "I heard losing weight helps people with anxiety. Why don't you just..."
- "Exercise is a great natural mood stabilizer. You should try..."[1]

These suggestions are sometimes kindly meant but rarely have a positive effect. Not because the information provided isn't accurate (though sometimes it very much is not), but because the underlying message that we are *fully* responsible for both our physical and mental health can fuel shame, self-loathing, and other toxic viewpoints.

And another, possibly more harmful underlying message comes along with: "I cannot accept you for who you are—here is information to help you become more acceptable to me."

This is fatphobia in action.

If you aren't already aware, please be advised that there is no singular choice a person with a mental health condition can make to cure themselves, just as there is no singular contributing factor to the state of our mental health. Are there choices we can make that could improve our mental health? Absolutely. Are there factors beyond our control impacting our mental health? *Absolutely.*[2]

Focusing exclusively on what a person can control can, rather ironically, limit their ability to control it. Feeling the full weight of responsibility for our physical and mental health, as if the functionality of our brain, body, culture, community, *and* thought processes is entirely ours to control, isn't empowering. Rather, it can be a crushing, paralyzing, and invalidating pressure that no individual should have to bear.

So let's discuss the ways in which external pressures that are beyond our ability to control impact our health, wellbeing, and sense of self.

THE FATPHOBIA-MENTAL HEALTH CONNECTION

i.e. How We Internalize External Messages About Our Worth

As mentioned in "The Brain-Body Connection" section, people with mental health conditions are routinely exposed to harmful stigmas, and fat people with mental health conditions are doubly vulnerable to these kinds of messages. They find us through innumerable channels including but not limited to:

- Opinions and suggestions of members, friends, neighbors, coworkers, random strangers, etc.
- Doctors and other medical professionals
- Popular entertainment—books, TV shows, movies, magazines, etc.
- Social media
- Shopping experiences (grocery, clothing, etc.)
- The size of seats and other aspects of private and public spaces (See Chapter 4 —Living in a Straight-Sized World)
- Our own thoughts, memories, and past traumas

All mental health conditions generally intensify when subjected to increasing pressure, and fatphobic pressures are certainly no exception. Here are some specific examples of how fatphobia could impact specific mental health conditions:

- Because of experiences with fatphobic individuals in the outside world, a fat person with agoraphobia becomes even more reluctant to leave the relative safety of their home.

- A fat person with clinical depression is constantly receiving messages from concerned friends with healthy recipes and other nutritional tips. The fat person's depression worsens because they feel they don't deserve medical care until they take their friends' advice, but their depression limits their ability to do so.

- While recovering from a past eating disorder, a fat person lapses back into self-destructive patterns after their romantic partner expresses attraction to a TV show character with a radically different body type than theirs.

Whatever degree of responsibility you believe someone has for their own physical and mental health, please give thought to contributing factors beyond your ability to perceive. It's entirely possible, and even likely, that the very thing you think they should do to improve their circumstances is not currently an available option.

> At the end of the day, fat people are people just like anyone else. Everyone deserves kindness and respect, to live their lives without fear of ridicule and judgement. Fat positivity isn't about "glorifying obesity," as so many trolls like to proclaim; it's about self acceptance and self love, and the desire to be treated fairly in the world."[3]

The toxic message that our worth as individuals is linked to our body shape and size can have a massively detrimental impact on our mental health.

While making choices that support our physical health can positively affect our mental health, this is only one of many contributing factors and should never be put forward as a cure-all. You can't cure anxiety by jogging. You can't cure depression with vegetables. A healthy sense of self-worth is far more crucial to our emotional, mental, and yes, even our physical wellbeing.

In removing fatphobic pressures and taking mindful steps towards acceptance, we give people space to figure out who they are and who they can become independent of pervasive shaming and blaming messages. If life is a garden, fatphobic messages are the strangling, nutrient-depleting weeds preventing us from achieving our full growth potential.

———

CHARACTER AND STORY IMPLICATIONS:

Give thought to how the intersection of mental health condition(s) and fatness make your character more vulnerable to societal stigmas related to both. Are they consciously aware of how fat shaming affects their mental health?

How do they feel when people give them "well-intentioned" advice about how to improve their health? Does it hurt them? Make them angry? Or are they more in a place of weary resignation at this point? How can their reactions to accidentally or purposefully shaming suggestions show readers the potential harm of these messages rather than continuing to normalize our cultural belief that fat people and people with mental health conditions need to be "fixed" and should be grateful for the help?[4]

Are there people in your character's life who bolster their sense of self-worth and accept them for who they are? Is your character aware of and grateful for their acceptance, or are they self-assured enough that this is normal to them?

How does your character's sense of self shift as their mental health worsens and/or improves? Does their ability to care for their physical needs shift as well? How can you show that there are mental health factors beyond their ability to control—that they are not fully responsible for the condition(s) affecting their functionality?

How can you show that your character has intrinsic worth that has nothing to do with how much space they physically occupy in this world, and/or how mentally well they are as they do so?

---

1. https://blogs.scientificamerican.com/observations/fat-is-not-the-problem-fat-stigma-is/

2. https://onlinelibrary.wiley.com/doi/full/10.
   1111/obr.12935
3. https://www.talkspace.com/blog/body-positivity-fat-
   acceptance-quotes
4. https://centerfordiscovery.com/blog/the-impact-of-
   weight-stigma-on-our-mental-health/

6

EATING DISORDERS AND BODY DYSMORPHIA

Content warning: this section discusses body dysmorphia and eating disorders in detail.

As discussed in Chapter 5, the mental health pressures of fatphobia can have a severely detrimental impact on any mental health condition. This is especially true when it comes to discussing body dysmorphia and its link with eating disorders.

When so many of the messages a person receives from society, medical professionals, and even loved ones tell them they need to be other than they are in order to be worthy of compassion, support, and respect, it's small wonder that some of us react to these pressures in ways that are deeply hurtful to both our minds and our bodies.

Whether you're writing a character who shares your own personal dysmorphia or eating disorder, or striving to include viewpoints outside your own experience, please take great care in incorporating these elements into your story. Each of these conditions has the potential to be life-threatening, and the way in which you depict them could either contribute to or reduce mental health stigma related to body dysmorphia and eating disorders.

What is Body Dysmorphia?

> Body dysmorphic disorder is a mental health disorder in which you can't stop thinking about one or more perceived defects or flaws in your appearance—a flaw that appears minor or can't be seen by others. But you may feel so embarrassed, ashamed and anxious that you may avoid many social situations.

> When you have body dysmorphic disorder, you intensely focus on your appearance and body image, repeatedly checking the mirror, grooming or seeking reassurance, sometimes for many hours each day. Your perceived flaw and the repetitive behaviors cause you significant distress, and impact your ability to function in your daily life.[1]

As with many mental health conditions, there are elements of body dysmorphia that likely sound familiar even to those who don't experience it at a debilitating-enough level for diagnosis. Most of us have some aspect of our body we're not entirely comfortable with, but body dysmorphia is more than wishing a certain body part weren't so prominent. It involves a sometimes disabling level of extreme preoccupation that makes it difficult to function. This may involve obsessive grooming behaviors, cosmetic cover-up and/or body modifying procedures, extreme mirror checking, and avoidance of social situations due to fear of ridicule and judgment.[2]

Body dysmorphia is never a given. Many fat people have an accurate, realistic, and self-aware viewpoint regarding their body shape and size. To assume that all fat people struggle with distorted perceptions of themselves strays into the realm of harmful stereotypes. Body dysmorphia can affect people of any size. It's a mental health condition, not a physical one. However, the pressure of living in a fatphobic culture can make fat people more vulnerable to this condition. Because society replicates body dysmorphia's harmful internal process and makes it external, whether fat people accept their bodies or not, societal narratives regard fat bodies dysmorphically.[3]

Anorexia is the condition most commonly linked with body dysmorphia, because many people on the outside are wondering how someone who is clearly underweight would see themselves as needing to lose weight. Because society prefers thin bodies, more people are able to see the body dysmorphia present in people with anorexia.

It's important to know that body dysmorphia can accompany any kind of body and any kind of eating disorder, but because our culture distinguishes between "good bodies" (thin ones) and "bad bodies" (fat ones), when fat people experience body dysmorphia, their extremely negative internal perception of their bodies matches society's extremely negative external perception of fat bodies.[4] Fatphobia means that thin people with BD will "deserve" a diagnosis, whereas fat people with BD may be ignored or even encouraged in it.

THE BODY DYSMORPHIA-EATING DISORDER CONNECTION

Eating disorders have multiple presentations, each with its own unique combination of contributing factors and symptoms, each taking an extreme toll on both the body and the mind. And while many assume that body dysmorphia invariably leads to restrictive eating disorders, it can be a contributing or exacerbating factor to other forms of eating disorders as well.[5]

For the purposes of this guide, we'll briefly discuss the following types of eating disorders. Note: *The Incomplete Guide to Writing Eating Disorders* will more fully address this topic.[6]

- Anorexia
- Bulimia
- Binge Eating
- ARFID

Anorexia

Anorexia nervosa is an anxiety disorder that includes compulsive behaviors (e.g. exercise, dieting) with obsessive ones (e.g., recording foods eaten, making calorie-dense foods for others.) This eating disorder often includes a distorted perception of weight, and is one of the conditions most commonly associated with body dysmorphia.

The most well-known symptom of anorexia is radically reduced calorie intake. There may also be a goal to lose weight or avoid weight gain, even in situations that warrant it (e.g. puberty, pregnancy, healing from illness). This kind of restricted intake affects how brains work, informing obsessions with food. This obsession has been replicated in starvation studies (Minnesota Starvation Experiment) to show the effects of starvation on the human psyche.[78]

 Anorexia isn't really about food. It's an extremely unhealthy and sometimes life-threatening way to try to cope with emotional problems. When you have anorexia, you often equate thinness with self-worth.[9]

You may be asking, "Why is a book on fat positivity including information about anorexia? That's a thin-people disease."

No, it's not. That's a myth. Fat people can have anorexia too.

Past criteria used to require a loss of 10-15% body weight for a diagnosis of anorexia nervosa, but that is no longer true. Not only can a person with any size body suffer from anorexia, atypical anorexia may be even more dangerous, as those with bodies that don't fit the popular conception of anorexic aren't tested for the markers of anorexia, and so symptoms like irregular heart rhythms or osteopenia go unnoticed and untreated. These conditions can worsen in response to this kind of fatphobic encouragement towards extremely restrictive diets and excessive exercise.

Anorexia is not a lifestyle or a diet; it's not a quirk or a character flaw. It's an anxiety disorder that affects people of any size, and can lead to a life-threatening mental and physical health condition.

Bulimia

Bulimia is most commonly known to include self-induced vomiting, but it includes any extreme measures a person may take to rid themselves of what they've eaten, or to prevent themselves from eating at all. These measures may include enemas, diuretics, laxatives, and extreme fasting, dieting, and excessive exercising. Lesser-known bulimic behaviors can include measures that may seem normal to those calibrated to our body-dysmorphic society, which are characterized as "dieting hacks," and can include purgative behaviors like chewing food and then spitting it out.

Bulimia intersects with binge disorder when eating large amounts of food is followed by feelings of guilt and shame and purgative behaviors. Bulimia intersects with anorexia when sufferers resort to extreme fasting and experience other symptoms of anorexia like obsessive calorie counting or creating lavish meals for others. This combined eating disorder is also known as bulimarexia.

 If you have bulimia, you're probably preoccupied with your weight and body shape. You may judge yourself severely and harshly for your self-perceived flaws. Because it's related to self-image—and not just about food—bulimia can be hard to overcome. But effective treatment can help you feel better about yourself, adopt healthier eating patterns and reverse serious complications.[10]

The diagnostic criteria for bulimia nervosa is:

"Recurrent inappropriate compensatory behavior to prevent weight gain, such as self-induced vomiting, misuse of laxatives, diuretics, or other medications, fasting, or excessive exercise. The binge eating and inappropriate compensatory behaviors both occur, on average, at least once a week for three months."[11]

Binge Eating

Sometimes presenting along with bulimia, binge eating disorder is the consumption of large amounts of food on a chronic basis. These behaviors are generally unrelated to physical hunger, and usually include an out-of-control feeling where a person who is in the middle of a binge may not know how to stop. Like all mental health conditions, stress is a contributing factor, including the mental health impacts of body dysmorphia.

Body Dysmorphia → Increase in Stress → Worsening Mental Health → Binge Eating Behaviors

The above pattern can become cyclical in nature, trapping the person in a self-destructive loop. This is important to acknowledge because our culture often resorts to shaming and rejecting people who don't have ideal bodies or ideal health, and this shame and rejection can increase the likelihood and severity of all eating disorders, including binge eating disorder.[12]

Like anorexia and bulimia, binge eating disorder is often used as a punchline or a shortcut to demonstrating inherent character flaws. Those who struggle with it are portrayed as being greedy, weak willed, and/or disgusting. The pervasiveness of this messaging is near inescapable, making it even harder for those with this condition to take positive steps towards better managing it.

Negative portrayals of binge eating disorder are usually based on a cultural narrative that relies on an inverse proportion between how much a person eats and how much they are worth and will likely be harmful for people who have any kind of eating disorder. Drawing these correlations between food consumption and personal worth does real damage to real people.

ARFID (Avoidant Restrictive Food Intake Disorder)

Often misclassified as "picky eating," ARFID is an eating disorder in which people are only able to eat a very narrow range of foods. With links to other mental health conditions and neurodiversities as well, reasons for food avoidance range from taste, texture, and smell, to extreme lack of interest or fear/anxiety reactions based on past negative experiences.

Sometimes, the person won't even be consciously aware of why they can't bring themselves to eat a specific food, making it even more difficult to address their food-avoidant behaviors.

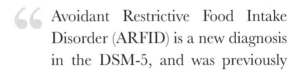 Avoidant Restrictive Food Intake Disorder (ARFID) is a new diagnosis in the DSM-5, and was previously

referred to as "Selective Eating Disorder." ARFID is similar to anorexia in that both disorders involve limitations in the amount and/or types of food consumed, but unlike anorexia, ARFID does not involve any distress about body shape or size, or fears of fatness.[13]

While diagnostically linked to severe weight loss, ARFID can also contribute to the kind of unhealthy eating patterns that lead to poor nutrition, binge eating, and ultimately weight gain. Difficulty with eating foods that are supportive of good physical and mental health can also incline those with ARFID to struggle with other health issues that can reduce their ability to maintain physical, mental, and emotional wellbeing.

Before you make that "picky eater" joke, give thought to the fact that it's not possible for an outsider distinguish between "pickiness" and a genuine mental health condition beyond the individual's ability to control.

CHARACTER AND STORY IMPLICATIONS

As you develop your character, consider who you want to portray as suffering from eating disorders and body dysmorphia, and why. Popular portrayals of eating disorders often differ based on common conceptions of who suffers from each kind of eating disorder, and how.

ANOREXIA AND BODY DYSMORPHIA ISSUES AND TROPES

Portrayals of anorexia nervosa have historically had a more sympathetic or tragic tone. These portrayals tend to highlight the body dysmorphia that many people with anorexia experience, showing a distressing difference between how they, the eating disordered people, perceive their bodies versus how society perceives them. These portrayals usually depict the anorexic perspective as subjective and mistaken, and society's perception as objective and correct.

Where this intersects with writing for fat positivity is this: the body dysmorphia that so often accompanies eating disorders often includes a terror of weight gain or being fat. To be very clear, society doesn't disagree with anorexia-related body dysmorphia that being fat is horrifying; it only disagrees that anorexics themselves are fat. Most portrayals of anorexia disapprove of the harm thin anorexics experience, but approve of these behaviors when people who aren't thin do them.

Some especially dangerous portrayals of anorexia in our culture romanticize or even approve of these behaviors, which has created a genre called "thinspiration" or "thinspo" where people encourage each other in self-harming behaviors. Again, these portrayals are based in a common fear and rejection of fatness. The idealization of health-endangering levels of underweight has accelerated since the late 1960s, but has historical antecedents in the romantic portraits of women wasting away from consumption (tuberculosis).

Be aware of these harmful—yet culturally lauded—approaches to body dysmorphia when-ever you consider portraying an eating disorder. Portrayals of anorexia that include bystander assurances that the sufferer isn't fat at all, but already beautiful and acceptable, will reiterate harmful concepts like "the only way to be beau-tiful and acceptable is to be thin" and "fat is ugly and rejected."

This fatphobic gaze also affects how our culture perceives depictions of anorexia-related restrictive dieting and extreme exercise. The difference is that our society generally feels these behaviors are unlivable for thin people, but approves of the same punitive practices when applied to fat people. One well-known example of this is the reality show *The Biggest Loser*, which we also discussed in the health section; this show simulates eating-disordered living for fat people, with predictably dangerous results for their long-term health.

It's absolutely vital to do the work to uncover the fatphobic bias in portrayals of all eating disorders, whether the sufferer's body is close to our society's idea, or far from it. This fat bias will reaffirm to all sufferers that being fat is a terrifying and unacceptable prospect, which can trigger or strengthen the fears that drive restrictions for all those with anorexia.

Portrayals that invalidate this experience —"what, THEY can't be anorexic, they're too fat"—can discourage people from seeking help when they desperately need it. This reaffirmation of fatphobia can make it exponentially harder for medical providers to recognize the danger atypical anorexics are in, and harder for those with atypical anorexia to access the care they need and to recover. Please don't add to suffering this way.[14]

.   .   .

Bulimia Tropes

Bulimia is often treated as a joke, frequently misused as a plot twist or a punchline. One trope is the joke about how a person should sneak into the bathroom to make sure their date isn't throwing up the expensive meal they just ate.

Another familiar trope is the popular mean girl who teases the nice fat girl; she later discovers the popular girl throwing up in the school bathroom, exposing her to the very mockery she's been dishing out.

Bulimia combines with misogyny and resentment when it's used in stories to humble characters, like a rich girl, or a successful businesswoman or celebrity. Making bulimia look like a disease of privilege affects marginalized people who struggle with it. These portrayals of bulimia often paint the disorder as something distasteful that justifies social ostracizing.

Making bulimia a character flaw contributes to the invalidation and stigmatization of those with bulimia, making bulimia seem both silly and gross, when in reality it's a serious eating disorder that can lead to long-term ill health.

Rarely do we see the other characters in the story express concern or offer support. Like all mental health stigmas, this further encourages those struggling with bulimia to hide rather than seek help. Give thought to this as you craft your stories. If someone with this condition reads your story, what will they be encouraged to do (or not do)?

BINGE EATING DISORDER TROPES AND CONCERNS

Binge Eating Disorder is the eating disorder that is most frequently attributed to fat people. There is a common misconception that the only reason a person might be fat is that they eat too much, and that they eat too much because of simple personal failings that are all too often treated as a self-explanatory punchline.

This misconception is based in a series of incorrect and harmful ideas. First, that being fat is an inherently disordered condition, and not a normal part of human physiological variety. Second, that being fat is a disorder, and one that results from overeating. Third, that solving the problem of being fat is simple: don't eat. Fourth, that because being fat is self-evidently a problem and because solving fat is simple, anyone who is still fat must either be fat because they choose to be fat (fat as moral depravity), because they are ignorant of the simple principles of weight reduction (fat as stupidity), or because they experience a compulsion to eat. Fifth, people have a moral duty to address this presumed depravity, stupidity, or compulsion with comments or instructions to lose weight. (This is how many people who bully fat people justify their criticisms as "concern for their health" or "sensible advice.")

This all-too-common stereotype of a fat person who binges dishonors both fat people and those with binge eating disorder, both through its reductive and disrespectful characterization of fat people, and also through its stigmatization of binge eating disorder.

This series of misconceptions plays out in many portrayals of fat binge eaters as gross slobs, people with emotional damage and dubious hygiene. Consider Fat Bastard, played by Mike Myers in *Austin Powers 2*. Fat Bastard's name is literally an insult that refers to illegitimacy, and the only time he breaks from being transgressive and encouraging horrified laughter through his appearance and poop jokes is when he engages in a sudden, tearful monologue about how he's fat because he eats to fill an emotional hole.

This conflation of being fat with binge disorder treats the eating disorder as a kind of fatness that needs to be addressed not only through physical diet and exercise, but through emotional diet and exercise as well—and that if a person doesn't "fix the problem," they're unacceptable.

Just like anorexia and bulimia, people with binge eating disorder come in all shapes and sizes.

Fat people do not all have binge eating disorder, and straight-sized people can experience binge eating disorder. Assuming fat people have binge eating disorder can lead people to tell fat people to stop eating. That's not only unhelpful to those fat people who do struggle with binge eating disorder, it's deeply harmful to fat people with anorexia or bulimia.

It's vital to the health and safety of those suffering from eating disorders that we strive as storytellers not to accede to popular and incorrect stereotypes of what eating disorder sufferers look like.

This is true for the portrayal of any health concern, but it's especially important for people struggling with eating disorders and body dysmorphia. It is crucial to their health and survival to have support in challenging their perception of their own bodies with a perspective that is inclusive and honoring, so that hopefully, stories that include eating disorders can support real sufferers in their journey toward healing.

While your story might not directly include binge eating disorder, be aware of how offhand comments about the quantity of food characters eat could be construed. For example, humorously equating the eating of an entire pizza with someone's social undesirability could reinforce deeply harmful stigma.

It's difficult to find fat representation in stories, and what representation exists is all too frequently a story about a fat person overcoming compulsive eating to become thin. These stories use binge eating disorder as a character flaw that a character must overcome, and often place fat characters in diet groups or fat camps to show them struggling with it. These stories are often told with a thin audience in mind, and confirm all kinds of harmful biases about fat people and compulsive eaters. Please don't do this. Don't use fat characters as a sideshow, or make their character arcs contingent upon them becoming thinner/more socially acceptable. This only serves to strengthen dangerous fat bias for fat people and stigma for those with eating disorders.

Questions to Ask Yourself

When considering writing a fat character struggling with an eating disorder, ask yourself these questions:

What about this story can only be told by depicting a fat person struggling with an eating disorder? What is the message I am hoping to send by portraying an eating disorder or body dysmorphia? What are the potential dangers, if I portray it poorly or harmfully?

What do I know about this eating disorder? Have I researched it and learned who suffers from it, and how? Do I see how thin privilege works against those who suffer from these disorders?

What do I know about cultural bias against fat people, and how that affects eating disorder development and body dysmorphia? Do I believe some bodies are wrong, or should be changed? Do I believe some people should engage in restrictive diets and extreme exercise, because of how they look? Do I understand the impact of these beliefs upon those with margin-alized bodies?

Who is my intended audience? How do I want to make them feel?

If my character has an eating disorder, how can I avoid harmful stereotypes? Do I know what the harmful stereotypes are? How can I show that eating disorders are valid mental health conditions in need of treatment and the supportive care of friends and family? How can I support those in eating disorder recovery and people in the fat community?

What contributing factors have impacted my character's mental health journey? How can I show my readers that these kinds of diagnoses are nuanced and multilayered?

Finally, in considering treatment options for your character, be careful not to present those treatment experiences as wholly harmful to your character. Yes, therapy can be uncomfortable, and it can be a struggle to find a therapist/pro-gram that's a good fit for your needs, but painting professional help in a severely negative light could discourage people from seeking desperately needed support.

———————————————

1. https://www.mayoclinic.org/diseases-conditions/body-dysmorphic-disorder/symptoms-causes/syc-20353938
2. https://www.nhs.uk/conditions/body-dysmorphia/
3. https://www.cci.health.wa.gov.au/Resources/Looking-After-Yourself/Body-Dysmorphia
4. https://www.eatingdisorderhope.com/information/body-image/body-dysmorphia
5. https://www.healthline.com/nutrition/common-eating-disorders
6. https://www.freedeatingdisorders.org/patient-family-support/types-of-eating-disorders/
7. https://academic.oup.com/jn/article/135/6/1347/4663828
8. https://www.apa.org/monitor/2013/10/hunger
9. https://www.mayoclinic.org/diseases-conditions/anorexia-nervosa/symptoms-causes/syc-20353591
10. https://www.mayoclinic.org/diseases-conditions/bulimia/symptoms-causes/syc-20353615
11. https://www.nationaleatingdisorders.org/learn/by-eating-disorder/bulimia
12. https://www.mayoclinic.org/diseases-conditions/binge-eating-disorder/symptoms-causes/syc-20353627
13. https://www.nationaleatingdisorders.org/learn/by-eating-disorder/arfid
14. https://www.nationaleatingdisorders.org/blog/top-5-myths-about-atypical-anorexia

7

RELATIONSHIPS

This section of the text is going to focus on fat people and relationships, primarily familial. We'll discuss romantic tropes in Chapter 10.

When you're fat, people think every "nice" thing they say about your weight is a good thing. Instead, they kick you in your jiggly butt and leave wounds you constantly have to hide and adjust.

I am fat. I have been fat all of my life. My family has been LARGE, LOUD, and LIVING IT UP for years.

I am comfortable with myself and wear my weight with pride, but a lot of this progress came from overcoming trauma and abuse, not from a loving and nurturing place.

In this chapter, we'll look at two of the most common problems within familial relationships around fatness: when loved ones speak harm, and when loved ones embrace harmful stereotypes.

WHEN LOVED ONES SPEAK HARM

I distinctly remember school clothes shopping with my grandmother, an old fashioned 1950s woman with a poodle skirt and sexism ingrained into her being. I was a big kid: 5'7 since I was in utero, broad shouldered (thanks, Father), a smooth 170 pounds, and what was then classified as a tomboy. Not to mention I was an emo kid with red-and-black straightened hair and eyeliner thicker than...well, me.

I was at Hot Topic with a budget of a hundred dollars. I was giddy with power, ready to buy what all the cool rich kids at school would sport —skinny jeans in every color. I was going to be stylish, and by God, trendy.

Being a big kid, I was mostly limited to my mother's hand-me-downs (Lane Bryant—God help the chunky twelve-year-old in a button-down and gaucho pants running around at summer camp) or boys clothes that were neither flattering nor looked good on my potato frame.

My grandmother, a well-meaning woman who wanted the best for me (but only if she liked it), looked over my shoulder and said, "Skinny jeans? The only reason you want skinny jeans is because it has the word 'skinny' in it."

Let's pause to focus on two elements of the story and their effect on me as a fat teenager.

1. The fact a loved one said fatphobic things is hurtful, period.
2. But my grandmother dug the knife a little deeper when she joked about the limitations that fat people have in clothing.

It's bad enough I was chubby in a time when it wasn't acceptable, but I had to look hideous while doing it? I just wanted to pick a struggle.

CHARACTER AND STORY IMPLICATIONS

Do not write your fat characters as if being skinny is the only goal. It is not a harmful stereotype to have a big person working out or mention that they want to lose weight, but it makes them one dimensional when those are the *only* things we know about them.

People who look like me are often placed in stories as a cautionary tale, not to make your writing more diverse or inclusive. A lot of characters are not given development and growth outside of their fatness.

I am more than being fat. I want the media to start reflecting that.

Fat is an adjective, just like tall, funny, or delicious. I can be all three.

Think of Traci Turblad from *Hairspray*. The premise of the movie is literally about accepting a girl because she's fat (which was to support a larger theme of inclusion and not being racist). Her mother constantly wanted her to be "NORMAL"!

My little ears heard that loud and clear: if you are FAT you are not NORMAL. This idea that fat is bad and thin is good has created eating disorders, dysfunctional relationships (I'm looking at you Celia from *Weeds*), and really bad jokes in the media from the 2000s.

Fatness is not wrong, bad, or a joke, and it's extra harmful when your family members are the ones who tell you that you are wrong, bad, or a joke. It's true in real life, and it's true for nuanced characters, too.

When Loved Ones Embrace Harmful Stereotypes

The irony in the story mentioned above is that my grandmother is also fat. In my years of memories of her, she has always been the round-faced Irish woman who fits the idea of Mrs. Weasley from *Harry Potter* more than Julie Walters did, but I'm biased. So you can imagine that added a further layer of salt to injury as another fat person, one of the few role models I had at the time, made a joke about my fatness. It also reflected the normalized internalized fatphobia that most bigger people hold unknowingly and then project onto others.

When considering relationship dynamics between fat people and their family members, let's look at *Kung Fu Panda* and the two father figures—Mr. Ping and Master Shifu.

Master Shifu's method of getting Po to be his definition of a warrior is through insulting him to the point where Po openly says, "Yeah, I know, I disgust you" to Monkey. Shifu even has Po train by having him catch dumplings and only through Po being a "flabby panda" does he work his way up to becoming the "Dragon Warrior."

In comparison, we have Mr. Ping's character, where the running joke of the movie is that everyone knows Po is adopted—but they are so close and look past each other's differences to the extent that no one ever mentions that Po is a panda and his father is a goose. Mr. Ping is supportive and understanding of his son's choices and never makes him feel like he can't be the Dragon Warrior because of his weight. In possibly the most important line of the whole movie, Mr. Ping tells Po that "To make something special you just have to believe it's special."

CHARACTER AND STORY IMPLICATIONS

Even if you are writing a narrative where the fat character has to overcome an obstacle relating to their fatness, don't let that obstacle be their family! It is a tired trope to have the fat character be shamed by *everyone* including their family.

There should be more examples of healthy dynamics that encourage and cultivate a healthy perception of the fat character, instead of constantly attacking them because of their size. Especially when most times it is read as a projection of the family's shortcomings and not the child's.

At the end of it all, why be mean when you can be kind? There are several ways to develop fat characters outside of their weight. It is harmful to see the few role models fat people have become tainted by how the people close to them react to their bodies. Especially when the assumption is that fat people are inherently unhealthy and lazy, which is only further confirmed because the only people put on this world to love and support them also treat them poorly based on their weight.

Be Mr. Ping, not Master Shifu.

8

GENDER BIASES AND
INTERSECTIONALITIES

F at people in any type of media are often described as "lazy," "pathetic," and "pitiful." Thanks.

However, this author is privileged amongst fat society because I got a couple of things going for me:

1. I'm a female-presenting person
2. Pretty (Hair flip, sis)
3. Hourglass shape
4. Willing to throw hands

Privilege is *anything* that makes my life easier because of what I look like (aka an aspect of my identity that is out of my control). Well, I am here to tell you that having these physical attributes has made my life easier in comparison to those who do not, and *that's* where privilege comes into play.

Society has deemed my body type more socially acceptable based on how much men want to sleep with me. I am tolerated more so in thinner circles because men are able to sexualize my body. So I'm good for something, right?

We see this on dating sites all the time—there's a fetishization for "thickums" and "thicc girls" but the equal and opposite reaction for "fatties."

There are oodles of examples of positive plus size, heavyset, big-boned, plump—or however you self identify—female-presenting characters. For example, Mindy from *The Mindy Project*, Tasty and Daya from *Orange is the New Black*, *Drop Dead Diva*, *My Mad Fat Diary* (that show got me through my teen years), and countless others.

Thanks to Lizzo and countless other positive role models in the media we have a choice in how we are presented. But if you notice, they are all female or female presenting. So don't we think it's about time we do the same for our male-presenting people and men?

Where My Chubby Dudes At?

Exploring the Lack of Plus-size or Fat Men or Male-identifying Characters in Media.

Research company *market.us* claims that over 25 million viewers watch Hulu, Netflix has 182.2 million subscribers, and there are 100 million Amazon Prime subscribers as of 2020. In sum, there are A LOT of people watching TV. Some titles that include heavyset men are:

1. *The Ugly Truth*: Katharine Heigl says my favorite lines as she explains to a colleague why they only hire fat weathermen: "If they get the forecast wrong, research shows people are more willing to forgive a fat guy."
2. *Norbit:* The literal whole movie is trash.
3. *Bob's Burgers*: They poke (sometimes literally) at the poor fat bald guy, Bob, every other episode.
4. *Avatar: The Last Airbender*: I hate to say this, but before Uncle Iroh got "SWOLE," they were constantly disrespecting my mans for being chubby. Even though he literally is called "Dragon of the West," but ok y'all.
5. *Kung Fu Panda*: When Jack Black is in a

movie, he is often the butt of every joke because he's a little chubby.

6. *Kevin James:* I was going to list one movie title but I can safely say, Kevin James made all his money on being the funny fat guy in films.

7. *Maaddddeeeeeaaaaaa...*

If you want more resources, **IMBD** has an article titled "Everyone's Favorite Jolly Fat Men"—basically the Fat Male Stereotype in one poorly written title.[1]

Look at the data collected—for the most part, if you are a male and fat, you'd better be funny, because that seems to be the only way society is going to embrace you. When the only fat male role models seen on TV are the funny fat guy, it is showing that their worth is in what you look like or what you can offer people.

Fatphobia is so ingrained into society, that most times we don't even know that a lot of the problematic jokes of the 90s to now still exist for fat people. We are the last group of people that you can openly make fun of without getting *too* much backlash.

Notice also that most of these roles mentioned in this chapter are side characters. If they are a main character, their weight is one of the most talked-about subjects of the show/movie.

This is the Jonah Hill Complex: he is the sidekick in most of his movies, even when he is the leading male actor because when you are fat and the script only gives you a one-note of humor, of course, he is typecast as the Leading Sidekick.

All the examples above are *recent*, too. Kivan, a twitter account, posted a perfect summary of this point: "Being fat is deciding to ignore fat hate on your favorite TV show because you tried giving up all the media that hates fat people once and there was nothing left."[2]

Character and Story Implications

In your writing, be conscious of how your male fat characters are treated. Are they treated "less than" *because* they are fat? Does the character have development? Is the only thing they talk about their weight?

Intersectionality—What if I'm a Woman, Queer, and Fat

There is a *severe* lack of queer fat characters. This is for a multitude of reasons: people don't like to see fat people, people don't like to see queer people, and we just barely started to give women character development outside of trauma. So HEAVEN forbid if you fall into one or of these character categories or identities or, like this author, are a Black Fat Queer Femme Person. I'm going to continue to exist whether society likes it or not.

I have only seen a handful of examples of a fat character having much background. There is a webcomic called *Big Jo* about a girl who struggles with her gender, weight, sexuality, and all the fun shenanigans of high school. She also comes from a culturally diverse household that for the most part loves her.[3] In the last few chapters, there is the introduction of a genderqueer fat Black woman. This was the *first time* I saw someone who *looked* like me or closer to what I look and act like than Rebel Wilson in *Pitch Perfect* (cringe).

Also, another awesome example is Spinerella from *She-Ra,* a show that has taken the queer community by storm because there are so many examples of healthy relationships. Spinerella, the WIFE (I know *WIFE*) of Netta, is a *powerful, respected, queer, fat* woman on a show that was targeted towards a younger demographic.[4]

Or better yet, *Steven Universe,* where every character has a *rich* background. One of the pivotal characters, Rose Quartz, is the subject of a song called "Giant Woman," a love ballad her partner wrote about him falling in love with an eight-foot plus-sized pink woman.[5] You truly cannot get more wholesome than that.

Character and Story Implications

If you do write a Black queer character (gender or sexuality), be really careful. You're dealing with two minority groups in this situation, and it's easy to slide into the White Savior role here. Always remember that whether or not you've perpetrated harm against these groups of people, if you are part of the biggest group harassing them, there is a very real chance of doing additional harm, even if it is unintentional.

We would invite you to consider these questions by author Alexander Chee:

1. Why do you want to write from this character's point of view?

2. Do you read writers from this community currently?
3. Why do you want to tell this story?[6]

If your goal is to come across as insightful and an advocate, you may be White Savior Complexing it. If you're not sure if that's what's happening in your piece, it's time to call in some diverse readers to help.

It is hard enough being fat in a world not made for fat people. It is *hard* being Black in a world that we made, but are denied access to at every turn. It is *hard* being queer in a world of hetero-normative culture.

So at the end of the day, I want to see me and people who look like me represented in a way that is respectful and accurate of everything that we are and can be. I want men, women, and all people to feel as if they have a place in the canon of media, because if we're not repre-sented, my assumption is that you don't want us there at all.

Don't just tolerate me, celebrate *all* of me.

---

1. https://www.imdb.com/list/ls000224089/
2. https://twitter.com/KivanBay/
   status/1005731690252128258

3. https://www.webtoons.com/en/romance/big-jo/list?
   title_no=854&page=1
4. https://www.teenvogue.com/story/she-ra-fans-defend-
   plus-size-spinnerella-following-fat-shaming-backlash
5. https://thetempest.co/2017/10/05/entertainment/
   steven-universe-body-positive/
6. https://www.vulture.com/2019/10/author-alexander-
   chee-on-his-advice-to-writers.html

9

GENERAL TROPES

Ah, the stereotypical fat character. They're a staple of modern media for the reason many other stereotypical characters are—people just love a good shortcut. If you overexaggerate one aspect of a character, it's easier to skip out on developing all the others.[1]

Hopefully, having read the previous sections of this guide, you're realizing just how damaging such shortcuts can be. In this section, we'll discuss a selection of common fat character tropes[2] for you to be aware of as you (fully) develop the fat characters in your stories.[3]

Fat to Serve a Purpose Tropes

You may notice a common thread running through this set of examples. These are the characters who exist in the story only to serve a highly specific purpose. As such, any quality or element of their character not related to that purpose tends to be poorly developed or completely absent.

Be careful not to send the (hopefully) inadvertent message that fat characters are only worth including as one-dimensional story props. Give thought to making sure your fat characters have an existence outside their service to your story. Like any well-developed character they should have their own goals and fears, motivations and limitations.

The Fat Lovable Mom Trope

This is a character who we love to love. She's the warm, nurturing, and self-sacrificing matriarch who helps form the heart of many beloved stories. As far as character tropes go, she seems pretty benign, right? Everyone loves the mom character who lives to feed, serve, and protect her dear ones.

But is that really all she's good for? Is that really the only kind of fat mom we're willing to accept and applaud? Is there room in our stories for the fat mom who's running her own business and forgets to make dinner? Or the fat single mom who's finding joy in exploring new romantic and sexual possibilities? What about the fat woman who chose not to have kids? Do we treat her like she hasn't achieved the measure of her creation, or do we love and accept her for the entirety of who she is?

Be wary of one-dimensional portrayals—even positive ones. If your fat lovable mom character fits certain aspects of this trope, consider how you can twist or build upon it. How can you show that she matters because of who she is, and not who she helps? Do the other characters in the story honor her sacrifices, offer care and concern to her, or support her in her own endeavors? Is she treated like a provider, or like the unique person she is?

THE FAT + SPECIAL SKILL TROPE

Often portrayed in comedic fashion, this character has unpleasant habits or qualities that make them an unwelcome addition to any team

—except for the fact that they have a special skill that makes them invaluable. And so, the team has no choice but to tolerate their flatulence, their theft of food from the communal kitchen, their poor hygiene and/or sweatiness, their persistent knock-knock jokes, etc.

One of the most common fat + special skill tropes is the hacker living in their parents' basement. They're presented as both physically and socially distasteful, but get to come along for the ride because they can hack into any system and provide the protagonist with vital intel. And they provide readers/viewers with comedic relief that can help defuse the tension during suspenseful scenes.

These characters are owed much and given little. As with all tropes, their personhood is minimized by the needs of the story. How might you change that? What additional positive qualities could you give them? How could you integrate them into the team in a meaningful way so they're not just tolerated, but instead accepted and maybe even respected?

THE FAT VILLAIN TROPE

More so than any other trope, the fat villain trope relies on the kind of false equivalencies discussed in Chapter 2. They are fat, therefore they are greedy. They are fat, therefore they are grumpy and unpleasant. They are fat, therefore they are damaged and prone to making bad choices.

This is lazy shortcutting at its finest/worst. Physical descriptions are often used to communicate the character's nature before any ill intent or bad action even takes place. The writer might take pains to point out the shape of their fat rolls and the way the chair they're sitting in can't contain them. References to food particles on their face and/or clothing might be used to show how greedy they are. And let's not forget the lovely addendum of personal hygiene, with mentions of sweatiness, greasy hair, bad breath, and flatulence.

If your villain is fat, be careful to show their villainy through their actions. Give thought to whether detailed physical descriptions might contribute to the kind of false equivalencies mentioned. Does the reader really need to find them physically distasteful in order to consider them a worthy adversary for the hero? What might it do for your story if the villain's physical presence were described in positive terms?

Fat Defines Them Tropes

Another common thread running through fat character tropes is the notion that the character must be defined by their size. Are these tropes authentic representations of some fat people's sense of self? Absolutely. Some tropes ring true! But this is where it makes sense for you to pause and ask yourself if these are messages you want to incorporate into your story or not. Knowing that many fat people have already internalized the hurtful and pervasive message that their value decreases as their size increases, do you want to reinforce that belief?

Our stories have the ability to echo reality—but we get to choose which echoes to share with our readers. As you consider the pervasiveness of some of these tropes, please give careful thought to whether you believe they should be echoed or not. And consider how reality can be impacted by fiction. What elements of fat positivity could you write into your story that might have a meaningful impact on how your readers perceive fat people? What echoes could you potentially set in motion?

THE PLUS SIZE TROPE

A character who is defined by their clothing size is a disturbing trend in modern media, but one that comes up often. A fat character will fondly reminisce about the time "when I was an [insert size]" or share heartbreaking tales of clothing store clerks giving them disgruntled looks, telling them "this isn't the store for you," or that their size is only offered online. Their sense of self-worth is tied up in the tiny number printed on a tag inside a piece of clothing they're hoping all the hopes will accommodate their body.

How might you twist this trope? Perhaps your story has clothing stores that are accepting and supportive of all body types? Maybe the sales clerk enthuses over how fabulous your fat character looks in a new outfit?[4]

THE FORMERLY FAT PERSON TROPE

This character is defined not by their current size so much as by their past one. We often see them gaze longingly at foods they've long denied themselves, fight internal battles as if giving into a momentary temptation might set them on a course back to a version of themselves they now repudiate, and sometimes pass hateful judgment on fat characters who have not yet achieved what they—through pure effort of will—were able to accomplish.

What's most harmful about this trope is that the possibility of getting fat again becomes the villain in their own personal story. To be fat is the very worst thing they can imagine, and the entirety of their identity revolves around a core belief that their worth is defined by what they are *not*, rather than by who they are.

How could this character's perspective of their past self yield a more positive impact? Do they really have to hate who they were to love who they've become?[5]

The Teaching People to Accept Them Trope

This is another particularly damaging trope. It's sourced in the belief that if a character cannot undergo a training/makeover montage and become miraculously slim and fashionable on the other side of it, then they must wage another kind of battle. Namely, they must convince people to accept and love them (see Chapter 7) for who they really are.[6]

These are the stories we call "inspirational." It's a rollercoaster of emotion as we watch the character persevere against prejudice as they rise up and succeed against the odds. These stories are considered overwhelmingly positive by many, so it might be surprising to learn that they can be intensely hurtful.

Let's use an analogy to illustrate how this trope can be problematic.

Picture a mountain. It's the tall, jaggedy type with lots of instabilities and very few handholds. Love, acceptance, and support wait at the top, as do all the people who were considered worthy of a free helicopter ride to the summit. The fat character doesn't get this automatic valuing. They must earn their right to stand on the mountaintop. And so they climb, and slip, and climb some more. They demonstrate their worth as they struggle and strive and ultimately succeed.

Battered and weary, they are welcomed and celebrated by the others on the mountaintop. Even though the character is fat, they have done great things. They have proven how smart, how driven, how successful they are, and have earned a place at the top.

But no one asks why they were left alone at the bottom of the mountain in the first place.

This is fatphobia in action, and stories of fat characters who finally earn love, acceptance, and support despite their size often serve to remind us how many people believe we weren't worthy of them in the first place.

There are always more mountains to climb, and we are tired.

Your stories can give fat characters free helicopter rides. You have that power. If you choose to leave them at the bottom of the mountain, why do you feel that's their place? Why do you want to tell a story where fat characters have to earn their belonging? Why not tell a story where they're fully developed and accepted human beings, treated by others how you yourself yearn to be treated?

And maybe, just maybe, you can find a way to let them fly the damn helicopter themselves.[7]

---

1. https://ca.style.yahoo.com/weight-and-bodies-in-literature-123743362.html

2. http://tvtropes.org/pmwiki/pmwiki.php/
   Main/HighFatIndex

3. https://self-publishingschool.com/character-
   development/

4. https://www.masterclass.com/articles/writing-tips-for-
   character-development#6-tips-for-writing-great-
   characters

5. http://www.writingeekery.com/5-dimensions-of-
   personality/

6. https://www.youtube.com/watch?v=L8uBTYRi9tY

7. https://youtu.be/xAgawjzimjc

10

ROMANTIC TROPES

Romance stories create a wonderful opportunity for meaningful and authentic fat-positive representation. This is because, all too often, fat characters are limited to being the sidekick or the comic relief. These kinds of harmful portrayals show fat people as mere types, people who only matter insofar as they're useful to the main characters of the story. In these depictions, fat people are defined by their appearance and what their appearance means in the gaze of others.

When a fat person is a lead in a romance, that already opens up potential for a fully realized character, rehumanizing a marginalized group that is often dehumanized. That's fantastic!

Here are some tropes to be aware of as you move forward with creating fat-positive romance portrayals.

Chubby Chaser

This trope is often played for laughs, because it's predicated on the assumption that of course fat people couldn't be attractive or sexy, and so someone attracted to a fat person is so outside the norm that their attraction is considered comic fodder, or maybe a fetish.

It's not transgressive to desire a fat person. Don't invite this idea on stage—it is based on the false belief that fat people are unworthy of love.

Can the one who pursues a fat character do so because they have a type? Sure! Many romance leads have a type, and that's a place to start. It's just not a place to stop.

Romances invite readers to identify with both leads. It's fine to have the initial spark be based in physical attraction. Fat people are both desirable and desired, and it's great to show that. Why and how does that emotional connection form? Don't skimp on this. Emotional connection is the key to creating a Happily Ever After that readers love.

Hot Guy Savior

Fat people are frequently marginalized, and that marginalization creates a power dynamic between the marginalized and the privileged.

Our culture unfortunately tends to define desirability as "would a man be sexually attracted to this?" Those who seek to hurt fat people (or any people, really) rely on this definition when they say things like "nobody would want to have sex with you."

This trope is based on an assumption that to be fat is to be automatically unattractive and unwanted, and fat women need to be grateful for any male attention they can get. This can create a story where a suffering fat girl needs to be saved from her own life, and where somehow she miraculously becomes worthy of attention from a man who's out of her league.

Some related portrayals will show fat people, especially women, as being in relationships that range from mediocre to abusive.

It's really important to note the intersection of male privilege and thin privilege here, and anticipate how it could intersect with other marginalized identities, including race and sexual orientation. Please be extra careful with how you handle these intersections. There are many negative stereotypes of fat Black women in particular that a wise writer will make themselves aware of.[1] (Check out our How to Write Black Characters for more information on that.)

Romance has already shown how to handle differences in power dynamics. Look at how many writers address economic disparities in the popular billionaire romance subgenre. It's a priority to show that the lead without the money is already worthy, and the growing romance often acknowledges the privileges and pressures surrounding having or not having money, but it isn't based on it.

This trope can also show up as Hot Girl Savior, where a fat guy is considered extremely lucky because a "hot girl" is attracted to him.[2]

THE MAKEOVER ARC

It's not uncommon for movies with romantic narratives to include parallel self-improvement arcs for one or both of the characters falling in love. But making the self-improvement arc about changing one's body can be hostile to readers who have similar bodies.

Stories with a weight makeover arc rely on an idea called "The Fat Has to Mean Something." That is, a character isn't just fat, they're fat because they're lazy and need a reason to get off the couch. They aren't just fat, they're fat because they're lonely outsiders who are bored emotional eaters. They aren't just fat, they're fat because they're mentally dull and don't understand nutrition until someone (usually someone thin) explains it to them.

Please don't make a fat character's weight their central conflict or motivation. It's rare to find positive fat representation at all, and it's even rarer to find fat representation that doesn't focus on the character's fatness. Weight loss and diet talk in a story is usually triggering for people with eating disorders and body dysmorphia. Steer away from this trope with both hands—readers are more than ready for stories that aren't about weight loss.

If you want to ground any character arc in self-improvement, please make it something other than a weight-loss journey. And please show how this character was innately worthy, all along.

———————

Makeover Arc: Male Lead

This variation on the Makeover Arc can be especially mired in sexist, heteronormative ideas of how romance is formulated. That is, the idea that men act, and women are acted upon. In this variation, weight loss becomes the quest male leads must undertake to prove their worth to the object of their pursuit.[3]

Romance should be a triumph, not a compromise. What kind of Happily Ever After is it to say, "Yeah, you didn't deserve much, so, be grateful for what you get"? No! Romance is about exhilaration and delight and desire and victory!

Romance writers, we can do better, and the best thing is, you already have the craft to do it. Just treat a fat person like they're already worthy of love.

I want to see characters whose fatness is not symbolic of anything. Characters who are fat simply because some people in the real world are fat . . . I like books that confront fatphobia head-on, and I'd also like to see books that aren't especially about fatness but that feature fat characters. Fat folks contain multitudes just like everyone else. Allow fat characters the humanity that not-fat characters have . . . Sometimes, as fits the story, let fat characters be happy and loved just as they are.[4]

Fat Gets in the Way

Every good romance has a meet-cute, obstacles, and a Happily Ever After.

I implore you: do not make fat the obstacle.

This says that fat people need to change to be loved; it says that it's right for society to refuse to love or even accept fat people.[5]

Think of how romance fans cheer for Pride and Prejudice's Lizzy Bennet when she turns down

Mr. Darcy's first fumbling and insulting marriage proposal, where he relates how he regrets his regard for her, and yet still loves her in spite of her and her family. We cheered for her refusal because that kind of conditional acceptance and arrogance is no solid foundation for a happy, healthy love affair.

But don't make their fatness the romantic obstacle. Doing so sends the implicit message that fat people are unworthy of love.

If your fat protagonist has to somehow earn their lover's regard, that's a toxic relationship and harms everyone reading it, especially fat people.

Don't let fatphobia get in the way of your readers' Happily Ever After.

Insecurity Gets In The Way

This is a variation on Fat Gets In The Way that borrows from the Makeover Arc. You can see this trope at work wherever fat people are instructed to solve problems by "having more confidence".

At first glance, this trope appears fairly benign--maybe even body-positive. It's great to have a break from the narrative that fat people need to purchase acceptance by changing their bodies; this trope instead tells fat people that they need to change their minds.

Confidence is great, and there are fat people we all know and love whose confidence is kickin', but you can't out-confidence systematic marginalization. And, in fact, criticizing marginalized people, and pointing to a presumed lack of confidence as the real obstacle, is an act of victim-blaming.

Marginalized people have a very logical reason to feel insecure: a lack of security. Fatphobia really exists and does real harm to real people. These repeated harms, unsurprisingly, lead people to feel insecure in situations that deny them security.

This trope says to fat people, "you know, if only you were MORE--more confident, more secure--then you'd be worthy! Sadly, you decided not to be awesome like that."

This also ignores the very real concrete manifestations of fat bias and sizeism in our society. Confidence isn't going to make an airline seat fit. Confidence isn't going to ensure a fat person has access to equitable medical care, employment, or clothing. Confidence doesn't make racism or sexism disappear. Confidence doesn't make fatphobic bias disappear, either.

It's no replacement for equal access and resources, and furthermore puts not only a burden of change on fat people, it can even invalidate that real marginalization exists, by invoking a presumed lack of confidence as the real problem, not actual obstacles like medical bias or obesity discrimination in employment.

These real harms cannot simply be magicked away with a pep talk, and telling a fat person to try has the effect of gaslighting ("those problems aren't real, they're just in your head") and victim-blaming ("if those problems do exist, and you feel bad about it, that's your fault").[6]

This is especially true if the person promulgating this narrative isn't fat. For a thin person to instruct a fat person to be more confident may be well-intentioned, but it's also thoughtless arrogance. For an author who isn't fat to use their story to instruct fat people that they just need to be more confident is more of the same.

Readers generally understand that thin people have real needs that cannot be addressed only via confidence; like thin people, fat people are also real people with real problems and real needs.

Gaining confidence is a valid character arc, but it's not a solution to systemic problems, and your audiences will find a story far more relatable and compelling and you more trustworthy as a story-teller if you make sure to authentically represent the real obstacles fat people face on a regular basis, regardless of their personality.

SHOULD I DEPICT FATPHOBIA IN MY ROMANCE?

Can you show a fat person dealing with cultural fat bias? Yes. Fatphobia is a real thing, and it can validate real fat people to see people dealing with it.

But there is a difference between showing fatphobia, and re-enacting it. One validates; the other harms.

We've talked a lot in this Incomplete Guide about the pain that societal fatphobia causes fat people, and how that is expressed in concrete things: things like poor mental health, medical bias, lack of access to seating in transportation and at public venues; "fat tax" in plus-size clothing. These are real things that cause real pain.

So, the first question an author may ask when considering how to write a fat character is how to portray this fatphobic reality. This question of authentic portrayal becomes doubly important in romance, because then one or both of the viewpoint characters is fat, and the experience of fat people moving through life will likely show up twice; first, through the perspective of the fat person experiencing life; second, through the perspective of the other character, who's falling in love with the first.

Acknowledging social stigma is one thing; reproducing the worst versions of it is another.

Harmful re-enactments can include publicly or privately humiliating your fat characters without redemption. This punches down on the marginalized and centers the story on trauma and pain, and this can have the effect of making readers feel bullied.

Sometimes writers will use trauma to create emotional intensity for readers. Please don't do this. Don't use the real pain fatphobia causes real people as a shortcut to create emotional intensity or conflict in your story. That's exploitative. Don't use realism as an excuse to beat up the people who come to your story for a Happily-Ever-After.

Storytelling is power, and it comes with responsibility. Using the pain of a marginalized community as a shortcut to emotional intensity is exploitative. When that happens, the book becomes the bully.

Make sure your execution matches your intention. If you feel that an authentic portrayal of a fat character requires showing them struggling with fatphobia, then include it. But if you do, please make sure that your story--whether through narration, monologue, or dialogue--addresses it with correction or contradiction so that your story can send a positive message that will make your story a safe haven for readers. Don't include one without including the other. Challenge the harm. Take your book from bully to best friend by caring for fat characters the same way you'd defend and redeem any other.

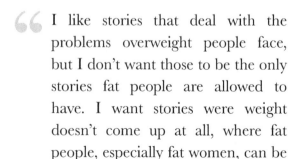 I like stories that deal with the problems overweight people face, but I don't want those to be the only stories fat people are allowed to have. I want stories were weight doesn't come up at all, where fat people, especially fat women, can be

cops or superheroes or love interests
or soldiers or princesses or anything
else we generally only allow thin
people to be.[7]

Fat representation means representation of all
things--not just trauma or pain, but also crushes
and joy and delight. We fat people have friends,
we have careers, we have torrid love affairs and
fun and commitment and lovers who enjoy us,
not despite our fatness, and not always because
of it, either. In short, fat people...are people.

The most important thing to remember when
writing a fat main character in a romance. Make
them people. Not a thin person in a fat suit, not
a problem to be solved, but people.

When you treat fat characters with respect, you
treat your fat readers with respect, too. Fat-positive representation in romance is how we can
teach each other that fat people deserve love.[8]

---

1. https://wearyourvoicemag.com/kim-parker-moesha-
   fatphobia/
2. https://pandabearshape.com/tag/character-tropes/
3. https://www.buzzfeednews.com/article/
   laurenstrapagiel/fat-women-love-interests-shrill-aidy-
   bryant-work-in-progress
4. https://www.thebooksmugglers.com/2016/07/trope-
   anatomy-101-body-not-confession.html

5. https://bookriot.com/fat-representation-in-romance/
6. https://www.thebooksmugglers.com/2016/07/trope-anatomy-101-body-not-confession.html
7. http://www.writingeekery.com/5-dimensions-of-personality/
8. https://threehousespress.com/2019/12/19/toxic-romance-body-types/

#WRITEDIVERSITYRIGHT PLEDGE

Join us on social media with your #WriteDiversityRight pledge. Tag us in your post—we want to hear from you!

I pledge to do my absolute best, do my due diligence, hire a sensitivity reader(s), and listen to and boost fat voices.

As a reminder, please remember to include content warnings when submitting materials to agents, editors, etc. Remember that they're human beings with their vast array of lived experiences and could be vulnerable in ways you might not be aware of.

AFTERWORD

Thank you for reading our Incomplete Guide! We hope you found it helpful. Please leave a review so that other people can find it.

You heard from many of our editors and readers in this book, and you've gotten a taste of what sort of people they are: kind, thoughtful, wise, and really, really cool. And best of all? They love stories.

Check out our wide array of readers at www. saltandsagebooks.com. Tell us that you came through the Incomplete Guide for a 10% discount.

You can find us on Twitter, Instagram, and Facebook—just search "Salt and Sage Books."

If you are a fat creator and would like to contribute to a future, expanded version, we want to hear from you! Reach out to hello@saltandsagebooks.com and use the subject "INCOMPLETE".

ADDITIONAL RESOURCES: BOOKS

Support your local bookstores and find these #ownvoices books here: https://bookshop.org/lists/fat-positivity-d4219fb9-52c3-4f95-9e03-9af4977b4a60

Fiction:

The Summer of Jordi Perez (And the Best Burger in Los Angeles) by Amy Spalding

If it Makes You Happy by Claire Kann

Fat Girl on a Plane by Kelly DeVos

I'll Be the One by Lyla Lee

Get a Life Chloe Brown by Talia Hibbert

Dumplin' by Julie Murphy

Leah on the Offbeat by Becky Albertalli

A Sisterhood of Secret Ambitions by Sheena Boekweg (2021)

Fat Chance, Charlie Vega by Crystal Maldonado (2021)

Nonfiction

The (Other) F Word: A Celebration of the Fat and Fierce (Anthology)

Body Talk (Anthology)

Fattily Ever After by Stephanie Yeboah

Fearing the Black Body: The Racial Origins of Fat Phobia by Sabrina Strings

Things No One Will Tell Fat Girls: A Handbook for Unapologetic Living by Jes Baker

Happy Fat: Taking Up Space in a World That Wants to Shrink You by Sofie Hagen

Shrill by Lindy West

Hunger: A Memoir of (My) Body by Roxane Gay

Hijas Americanas: Beauty, Body Image, and Growing Up Latina by Rosie Molinary

ABOUT THE AUTHOR

Salt and Sage Books is an editing company centered on the idea that a rising tide lifts all boats.

We are a creative community of devoted readers, writers, and editors, hailing from the desert's sunwashed sage to the coast's shining seas, and we've brought together our diverse skills and experiences in a single welcoming place, to help writers like you.

When you choose Salt and Sage, you join a creative community working together to change the world through story.

Check out our Incomplete Guides series for an accessible first step into writing diversely.

You'll find a wide range of editors, sensitivity and expert readers, and beta readers on our website, www.saltandsagebooks.com.

Welcome to the rising tide.

How to Write Atheist Characters

How to Write Intersex Characters

How to Write Latinx Characters

How to Write Queer Characters

How to Write Characters from the U.K.

How to Write Characters from Spain

How to Write about Anxiety

How to Write about PTSD and Trauma

How to Write about Therapy

And more!

If you'd like to see one of these guides sooner than another or have ideas for another guide, please email us at hello@saltandsagebooks.com.

Made in the USA
Las Vegas, NV
24 March 2021